# Small-Scale Mode

C000183294

# Small-Scale Modelling

## Caroline Osborn

The Crowood Press

First published in 2000 by
The Crowood Press Ltd
Ramsbury, Marlborough
Wiltshire SN8 2HR

© Elizabeth Caroline Osborn 2000

All rights reserved. No part of this publication may be reproduced or transmitted in any form or by any means, electrical or mechanical, including photocopy, recording, or any information storage and retrieval system, without permission in writing from the publishers.

**British Library Cataloguing-in-Publication Data**
A catalogue reference for this book is available from the British Library

ISBN 1 86126 228 0

All photographs by Ken Osborn.

**Acknowledgements**
Anna Lamour for plasterwork throughout the book; Apollo Miniatures for furniture supplied as whitewood and used in projects throughout; Basique for cake-top figures used in the Cabinet House Garden on pages 61 and 125; Bryan Frost for house and room boxes on pages 14, 43, 52, 53, 115 and 127; Cel Craft for cold porcelain paste, moulds, cutters and tools; Clive Brooker and Carol Mann for pots and dishes used throughout; Dolls' House Direct (Wales) for resin furniture used in half scale hotel, Georgian house and ¼ scale shops – Tea Kiosk, Beach Hut and half scale hotel on page 139; Dolls House Emporium for accessories and furnishings throughout and also the Manor House which started all this; Duncan Ceramics Moulds for moulds used in the photographs on pages 7, 8 and 164 (Baptist Chapel); fabrics and trimmings obtained from North London Fabric Warehouse, Hilda Burden Fabrics, Dixie Collection, Dolls' House Draper and Tee Pee Crafts; Freda's Cakes for cake topper used in Cabinet House as wedding couple and terracotta flower pots; Garden Railway Supplies for motor bikes and figures on page 24, pub supplies and garden furniture in hotel; Gare Ceramics for greenware Victorian lady in photograph on page 45; Harrow Model Shop for modelling materials used throughout the book and for the Market Stalls photographs; Hobby's for dolls' house kits used on pages 9, 95 and 105; HobbyCraft Superstore for papier mâché shapes and craft supplies used throughout the book; IKEA for room boxes on pages 110,112 and Tea Lady on page 147; In Some Small Way for musical instruments in Party House and furniture in Country-Style Shop and Alchemist's House; James Hickling for the Cabinet House; Dolls' House Shop, Lincoln for ¼₄ model houses on page 9;

Maple Street for accessories and carpets; Masters Miniatures for furniture on page 159; Phoenix items supplied by JoJay Crafts; Pixie Rusties for the Sweet Stall on page 145; Poppy Ceramics for ceramichrome mould greenware for Mouseville, Count Dracula and Painted Lady; Prime Properties for the vegetable stall on page 103; Renee Stubbs for furniture shown in photographs of Alchemist's House on page 137; Sue and Alan's Little Treasures for pub on page 32 and room box on page 118; Sid Cooke for shops on pages 18, 106, 107, 108 and 109; Tom's Miniatures for houses on page 113 and basic garden in 'My Garden'; Tudor Time for chest shown in Alchemist's House bedroom on pages 137–8; Two Hoots, Guildford for greenware ¼ scale houses on page 85; Valerie Claire Miniatures for labels, groceries, jars, bottles and miniature goods used throughout; Veronique Cornish, Sadie Jocelyn and Glasscraft for ornaments throughout; Wendy's Dolls for Tom and Sophie in Georgian House on page 126.

The following companies have given their permission for Valerie Claire Miniatures to miniaturize some of their brand label products and these are photographed throughout the text. Bisto Foods, British Birds, Brocks Fireworks, Coates Crafts, Elida Gibbs, Gerber Foods, Interflora, Kraft Jacob Suchard, Lever, McDougalls Foods, Penguin UK, RHM Foods, SmithKline Beecham, Taylors of Harrogate, Tesco Stores, Trebor Bassett, Warner Lambert Confectionery, Nestlé Rowntree Products, packaging and associated trademarks and copyrights reproduced by permission of Société Des Produits Nestlé S.A.

Individual artists are acknowledged in the text.

I would also like to acknowledge the contribution made by my husband, Ken, who took the photographs and my secretary, Sheila Martin, who typed the manuscript. I'm also grateful to my Editor, Julie McRobbie, for her patience and understanding, and to Marion and Edward Fancey and all the staff at *Dolls House and Miniature Scene* for their encouragement and advice.

Typefaces used: New Baskerville (*text*); Optima Bold (*headings*).

Typeset and designed by
D & N Publishing
Membury Business Park, Lambourn Woodlands
Hungerford, Berkshire.

Printed and bound by Leo Paper Products, China.

# Contents

# Introduction

My first dolls' house was made out of orange boxes. As an army child, I quickly learned that small was beautiful because it was easy to pack. Small treasures were easier to carry and less likely to go astray since I could fit them all into the small suitcase that the Ministry of Defence allowed as hand luggage. The orange boxes changed each time we moved. Ghee tins in India, splendid silk-covered boxes in Hong Kong, baskets with lids, even an ornate little cupboard in Germany, were pressed into service. My father was a collector himself and indulged me with approval and strange little gifts from his travels. My mother loved to make things and passed this passion on to me. Each time we moved, my little houses, like our army accommodation, were left behind but their inhabitants and possessions came with us.

There was a lull in this consuming passion for miniatures to take in school, university and the beginnings of my professional life as a solicitor, not to mention my family. However, you can't keep a good miniaturist down and I married a railway modeller. My husband models in EM gauge, 4mm scale, and I have adapted another hobby, ceramics, to make interesting and cheap houses for his layouts. There are, however, limits to the number of houses, people, castles, trees and other non-railway items which even a doting newly married husband will allow on his layout and we are well past our silver wedding anniversary …

Partly to keep me away from his layout and partly to provide solace during a particularly loathsome bout of 'flu, Ken gave me a dolls' house kit and then a subscription to a magazine.

*Cottage made for railway layout.*

*Old mill made for railway layout.*

As a practising solicitor, I don't propose to admit to how many dolls' houses, room boxes, books, back numbers of dolls' house magazines, bits and pieces waiting to be used, kits and half-finished dolls share the house with us, three cats and the research for my next book. You really wouldn't believe me if I told the truth.

My models have stories attached to them. There is the alchemist's house, John Wellington Wells' magic emporium, with apologies to Gilbert and Sullivan, VE night complete with the occupants' fantasies about food and post-war life, a scruffy café with Hell's Angels, shops for books, food, crafts and car repairs. The occupants are not all human. They range from witches to wizards, extraterrestrials to animals, glamorous ladies in ball gowns to a fat lady buying ice cream.

I make and collect. I prefer to use half-inch to the foot scale ('half scale') because there is still space for detail in the actual objects I create, but enough room in our human house for my grandiose schemes. I have no loyalties to any particular time or country. Ancient Egypt and Dr Who have made guest appearances in my collection. Half scale is very flexible. I have cats, dogs, horses, mice, rats, jackdaws, dragons, elves, hobbits, ghosts and, indeed, dolls for dolls' houses. I do have projects in $\frac{1}{2}$ scale as you will see from what follows, but I also model in other scales including some of the uncommon ones down to $\frac{1}{144}$ scale, which is a particular favourite.

Two years ago I was asked to write a column for *Dolls House and Miniature Scene*. This grew to be a regular feature. I can only convey unbounded thanks to Marion Fancey and her staff for their encouragement. I also write occasionally for *Dolls House and Miniature Scene*'s sister magazine, *Dolls House Projects*. I have also conducted a number of very informal workshops, principally to teach the techniques for modelling with cold porcelain. I don't plan to give up on my day job, but modelling has provided me with all sorts of interesting projects and challenges and, most importantly, many friends.

The purpose of this book is to give you a guided tour of my miniature kingdom and some special projects, DIY tips and techniques to use in your own miniature worlds.

# Scale and Practical Matters

## SCALE

Miniaturists, collectors and modellers, both professional and amateur, tend to have a preferred scale. Whether you wish to produce a completely accurate replica or a fantasy, scale is important. Models are usually smaller than the original. The exception is the kind of model that is built for educational or instructional purposes, such as models of the human eye and brain. For most people, miniaturization is one of the key attractions of the hobby and, indeed, of professional modelling.

Scale determines the proportional relationship between the components of a model. In simple terms, if you model a

*Dolls' house shop interior.*

shop, it makes sense to have a shopkeeper who fits in with the shop fittings and the stock. A shopkeeper made in $\frac{1}{12}$ (one inch to the foot) scale would look like a giant in a $\frac{1}{24}$ (half an inch to the foot) scale shop. There may, however, be occasions when you wish to exploit disparities in scale. On page 9 there is a dolls' house shop where the shop is made from a $\frac{1}{12}$ scale wooden kit. The stock inside this shop is dolls' houses, dolls and accessories. In $\frac{1}{12}$ scale, dolls' houses work out as houses built in $\frac{1}{144}$ scale (which equates to 'N' gauge in model railway terms). Most collectors and modellers swiftly discover that in an average-sized house (including full-size humans), three or four $\frac{1}{12}$ scale houses are delightful. Twenty is an embarrassment of riches and suggests it is time to open a museum.

It may not be possible to build some projects in $\frac{1}{12}$ scale because of the space required for building and setting up. Better, therefore, to choose one of the smaller scales of $\frac{1}{24}$ or $\frac{1}{48}$ ($\frac{1}{4}$in scale).

Below I set out the scales commonly used for various common areas of modelling. Scales evolve in use for a variety of reasons. Some are scientifically calculated to give the best combination of size and detail accuracy whereas some happen more or less by accident. British modeller James Hay Stevens was responsible for the now universal $\frac{1}{72}$ scale for model aircraft. He assumed that the lead soldiers he purchased were $\frac{1}{36}$ scale although in fact they were the more common $\frac{1}{32}$ scale and he halved that scale for convenience. His commercial venture constructed wooden model aircraft kits to this scale and everybody else followed suit.

The popular scale of $\frac{1}{32}$ scale evolved from early tin plate train sets which were made to fit in with the existing ranges of lead model soldiers and farm scenery. $\frac{1}{32}$ scale was called '1' gauge. Larger models, not surprisingly, became known as '2' gauge. A smaller scale of 7mm to the foot or approximately $\frac{1}{4}$ scale was called 'O' or

'Zero' gauge. That gauge was in turn halved to become 'Double Zero' or '$\frac{1}{2}$ Zero', commonly called 'HO' or 'OO'.

The most common commercially used scale for dolls' houses is one inch to the foot. This is in common use in Europe and America. More recently, there has been a flurry of activity, much to the surprise of model railway addicts, of smaller scales. These are half scale, quarter scale and $\frac{1}{144}$ scale.

## TRAINS

Model railroads are produced to well-established scales, and the track gauges are usually linked with them. But gauges can vary, especially in the case of narrow-gauge models. Almost any plausible combination of scale and gauge is possible. Only the smaller scales and gauges suited for indoor use are covered here.

- 1:22.5 scale/G gauge. The largest commercially produced size, depicting narrow-gauge trains and 1¾in (45mm) gauge track. Some scale variations are possible, depending upon the full size gauge that 1¾in is taken to depict.
- 1:32 scale/1 gauge. Standard gauge trains on 1¾in (45mm) gauge track. Some 1:30 scale is used.
- 1:43.5 scale/O gauge. Standard gauge trains on 1¼in (32mm) gauge track. In the United States, the scale used for this gauge is 1:48, or ¼in (6mm) to 1ft, and in mainland Europe it is 1:45.
- 1:64 scale/S gauge. Standard gauge trains on ⅞in (22mm) gauge track. Popular in the United States.
- 1:76 scale/OO gauge. This is a peculiar British variation on HO, where the body scale of the models is slightly enlarged but the models still run on ⅝in (16.5mm) gauge track, which is under-gauge for the scale. To correct this, some dedicated British modellers alter the gauge to 18.2mm (EM gauge) or 18.83mm

(P4/S4), which are more accurate renditions of the gauge.

- 1:87 scale/HO gauge. Standard gauge trains on ⅝in (16.5mm) track. The most widely adopted scale in the world: about 80 per cent of all railway modellers use this gauge.
- 1:120 scale/TT gauge. Standard gauge trains on ½in (12mm) gauge track. There is a British variation of 1:103 scale running on ½in gauge track, repeating the same scale/gauge error as noted with OO gauge.
- 1:160 scale/N gauge. Standard gauge trains running on 1⅙in (9mm) gauge track (a scale of ⅙in to 1ft). After HO, this is the most popular scale. There is a British variation of 1:148 scale and the Japanese variation of 1:150 scale on the same track gauge. Both of these give larger scale bodies on the same track gauge and therefore offer a slightly inaccurate scale/gauge relationship.
- 1:220 scale/Z gauge. Standard gauge trains running on ⁹⁄₃₂in (6.5mm) gauge track; the smallest commercially supported model rail scale.
- Narrow gauge. There are many possible combinations. Typical is HOM, where models to 1:87 scale run on ½in (12mm) gauge track, depicting metal gauge. Similarly Nm uses 1:160 scale trains running on 6.5mm (Z) track depicting metal gauge trains. HOe has models to 1:87 scale running on 9mm (N) gauge track, depicting 750mm narrow gauge. There are many others and in essence the scale is paired with the most appropriate gauge that is to be depicted.

In the United States the most common variations of narrow gauge, apart from G scale, are HOn2½ (using 9mm/N gauge track to depict 2ft 6in gauge), HOn3 (using 10.5mm – 1⅜in – gauge track to depict 3ft gauge), On2½ (using 16.5mm – ⅝in – HO track to depict 2ft 6in gauge) and

On3 (using 19mm – ¾in – gauge track for 3ft gauge).

## AIRCRAFT

- 1:24 scale. A limited number of giant 'super kits' are made in this scale, covering the most famous fighting aircraft such as the Spitfire, *Stuka* and P-51 Mustang. Their size can make them vulnerable, but the completed models are most impressive.
- 1:32 scale. Several manufacturers have plastic kits in this large scale, where every detail, inside and out, can be featured. As for the 1:24 scale, the finished models can pose a storage problem.
- 1:48 scale. Sometimes known as 'quarter scale', that is, ¼in to 1ft. This gives scope for fine detail on a larger model and is the next favourite scale after 1:72.
- 1:72 scale. The most popular scale, with hundreds of plastic kits from many manufacturers. It is a convenient scale, working out at 6ft to 1in.
- 1:144 scale. Arrived at by halving 1:72 scale – therefore, 1in to 12ft – this gives very small models, which are easily stored and displayed. These supplies are suitable for dolls' house dolls.
- 1:200 scale. The smallest scale, favoured by collectors. Plastic kits and models of large airliners are often to this scale. Specialist suppliers make cast-metal aircraft (including fighters and bombers) at this scale, and these tiny models have exquisite charm.

## CARS

- 1:18 scale. Several super-detailed die-cast car ranges are made in this scale.
- 1:24 scale. Some die-cast models and kits are available in this large scale.
- 1:32 scale. Many plastic kits and some die-cast models are to this scale, which matches gauge 1 model trains.

- 1:43 scale. The most popular size for die-cast automobiles with many companies producing an ever-changing range of models at all prices. Some plastic and metal kits are also suitable. The scale matches European O gauge model trains.
- 1:87 scale. Many American and European companies produce thousands of models in this scale, which matches HO trains. It has become a popular collecting scale in recent years, especially in continental Europe, even though the models were originally produced merely as rail accessories. There are numerous plastic kits and some metal ones. Heavy trucks and buses are popular in 1:87 scale. The models are well detailed but occupy minimal space.
- 1:160 and 1:120 scales. Some 1:160 scale models are produced in support of N gauge and 1:120 road models are made for TT.

## MILITARY MODELS

- 1:32 scale (also known as 54mm scale). This is the standard model soldier size, well supported, with ready-made, cast metal, plastic and kit models. Armed forces vehicles are also modelled to this scale. Figures are 2¼in high. Historically accurate furniture and accessories are available in this scale.
- 1:35 scale. Though a slightly odd size, this is a well established scale for large military vehicle models that originated in Japan. It is just below the 1:32/54mm scale that has been standard for model soldiers for over 100 years. Many plastic kits and accessories are available in this scale, and it is extremely popular for its bulk, fidelity and high degree of detail.

Model figures for collectors are also produced in 3¾in, 2¾in, 1½in, 1¼in and 1in (90mm, 70mm, 40mm, 30mm and 25mm) size, the smallest equating to HO and OO gauge model railways. Many armoured vehicle kits and models are available in 1:87 and 1:76 scale – the latter is favoured by collectors of military vehicle models.

## SHIPS

Most ship models are made to fairly small scales. There is some variety among models made from plastic kits, because manufacturers tend to scale them to fit conveniently sized packages. However, the following are well established:

- 1:700 scale. This scale was standardized by several Japanese kit makers to produce a high-quality range of waterline warship models. There are many kits, and this is a good scale for the collector. A few models and kits are made to 1:720 scale, which is visually compatible in this small size.
- 1:600 scale. This is a well-liked scale – 1in to 50ft (25mm to 15m) – with a fair range of plastic and wooden kits.
- 1:1,200 scale. This is a long established 'recognition' scale – 1in to 100ft (25mm to 30m) – favoured by scratch builders but also supported by some plastic kits.

There are also kits in 1:50, 1:150, 1:200, 1:300, 1:350 and 1:400 scale, among others.

A final point on the practical point of scale: scale rulers can be bought from modelling shops and can be very useful, particularly for beginners who may not yet be familiar with the look of their particular preferred scale.

# THE ADVANTAGES OF SMALLER SCALES

Some of the advantages of using small scale are pretty obvious. For example, less material is used: a Georgian tea kettle made in ½ scale may use just as much skill, but the troy weight of silver will be so much less as to

# Health and Safety Matters

It is all too easy to forget in experiencing the pleasure of small-scale modelling that some of the products we use can be very dangerous if not treated with respect, as indeed can the simplest of tools. Please remember the following:

- Paints, adhesives and solvents may be dangerous to health and also flammable. Read the directions on the container and follow them scrupulously. Do not smoke. Do not spray paint or adhesive near any sort of naked flame. In particular, airbrushes and aerosol cans of paint, varnish and adhesive are better used out of doors. Even the empty containers should be treated with respect: they can explode. Follow the manufacturer's directions for disposal.

- Keep your modelling materials, tools and projects away from small children and pets. You will have noticed that many miniatures sold commercially bear warnings in accordance with the law concerning toys. I am well aware that there are many young modellers who resent being, as they see it, excluded from the hobby. You owe it to them to teach them safe practice and to ensure that they understand why this is necessary.

- Use tools for their intended or instructed purpose. Follow the manufacturer's instructions.

- Do not work in an overcrowded or badly lit area.

- It is good practice to invest in a pair of safety glasses and a safety mask, particularly when working with metal, wood, glass or other products which may pose danger to your sight or create dust. These items can be obtained from DIY stores and ironmongers.

- Keep your tools sharp, protected and in a toolbox, not loose on a work surface where they may roll off. Tidiness equals safety.

- Use sharp tools such as knives and saws, so that they are pointing away from your body.

- Keep your hands and feet well clear of any drill and observe recommended safety standards with power tools.

- Always use sharp knife blades and do not force a knife, particularly through plastic or metal – this may cause the blade to shatter.

- Tie your hair back if it is long and do not wear loose jewellery or clothing which may get caught, particularly in power tools.

- Dispose of dangerous waste such as old paint cans or old, supposedly blunt, blades from modelling knives in a responsible manner. Aerosol paint cans and left-over solvents and paint can be disposed of on Council rubbish tips. Glass should be wrapped before it is put in the waste bin and old blades should be disposed of in a suitable receptacle. Either obtain one from a medical supplier or use an old plastic box or biscuit tin with a slot cut in the lid. Needless to say, this should be kept well away from children.

- Always use a firm cutting surface and clamp work which is to be cut. Self-healing cutting mats are advised.

*Tudor village.*

make the item a great deal cheaper. The same is true for houses and furniture. Expensive products such as gold leaf can be used quite lavishly where they would be wholly inappropriate in full size. The array of silver and china shown in the dining room of the cabinet house portrayed on page 119 is appropriate to a stately home, and also a frightening responsibility to insure in full scale. Many items are attractive to collect in miniature but impossible because of their fragile nature in full scale. As must be

obvious, small-scale modelling from half scale downwards allows a larger collection. Eight half scale houses will fit into the space occupied by one ½ scale house.

There is a great deal of cross-fertilization with other hobbies. Model railway suppliers carry a huge range of architectural fittings, such as cornices and windows, that can be easily converted for use in houses and, indeed, in furniture. Many of the small nick-nacks which convert a half scale dolls' house from model to masterpiece are readily available in the plastic kits sold for railway modellers. Examples of these are bottles and glasses for public houses, tools and even a wide range of people.

There is also, because railway modelling and other mechanical modelling has been popular for so long, a wide range of relevant literature, and magazines which contain articles of use to the house modeller. A bibliography appears at the end of this book and there are references to particular items of interest in the text.

Much larger projects are possible. Towns, streets, fairs, markets, car showrooms, ports, canal ways and elaborate Christmas settings can be constructed in half and quarter scale which would be completely impossible in $\frac{1}{12}$ scale. My complex projects on pages 157–66 illustrate this.

Smaller scales allow cross-fertilization between scales. $\frac{1}{32}$ scale is one of the oldest scales used for lead soldiers, farm animals and other serious modelling, particularly of the sort used in films before computer graphics were invented. Many of the products made, for example in the Phoenix range of furniture, transfer well from $\frac{1}{32}$ scale to half scale. Toy soldiers are fun to paint and add a touch of colour and class to models. They also fill a gap: my experience is that it is nearly impossible to produce a well-cut suit for a doll in $\frac{1}{2}$ scale. In lesser scales, fabric is a non-starter. Modelling in white metal or other media such as Milliput is the only answer (*see* the Sherlock Holmes Room on page 115).

# STORAGE

It goes without saying that storage for tools, materials, work-in-progress and bits and pieces is important. As a whole, miniaturists range from organized chaos through to an incomprehensible mayhem in which only the miniaturist concerned can find anything. Here are a few golden rules:

- Damp is a great enemy. Materials, fabrics, ribbons, sewing cottons and so on will become musty and eventually mildewed. They need to be stored somewhere dry and dark. Paper, as the curator of the Prints Department of the Victoria and Albert Museum will tell you, becomes damaged much more quickly. It will exhibit brown marks, sometimes called 'foxing', which are caused by a mixture of damp and human touch. I store large pieces of paper in a roll secured with masking tape and small bits, like writing paper, flat in a box file. It is possible to iron creases out of paper but with more delicate products, such as some dolls' house wallpapers, this may result in a loss of colour. Test a small piece first. Hardware, such as wire, white lead, models, porcelain doll parts and other relatively robust items are kept in small boxes which, in turn, are stored in vegetable racks. I also use plastic stacking boxes with lids. My workbench, which is portable, came from Lakeland Limited.
- Paints, solvents and glues can be dangerous (*see* page 13). They should be stored somewhere cool and dark, away from naked flames, and from children and pets.
- Every modeller needs their own place, even if this is only a portable modelling bench which has a cutting board as a integral part with storage underneath. A modelling room of one's own makes for a happy marriage and family life. I suspect that I live in a modelling house. What do you expect with two keen miniaturists in the same family?
- Attention should be paid to health and safety particularly when dealing with clay, adhesive, paints and sharp tools (*see* page 13).

# — 2 —

# Designing a Project

Like most collectors who are also part-time modellers, I drool over the work of really talented craftsmen. The only way in which I shall achieve a Georgian Manor House, a Fairy Palace or Tapestry Chairs from Fontainebleau is to struggle to make them myself. For some reason, many of the ladies who write to me as a result of my regular column in *Dolls House and Miniature Scene* are frightened of designing their own projects or even of adapting non-copyright plans and drawings. There are a great number of well-written and beautifully illustrated books for the ½ scale miniaturist. A list of some of these appears in the Bibliography. To assist small-scale modellers I set out here the ways in which a pattern can be enlarged or reduced from, if necessary, even a life-size drawing.

The first method of reducing a pattern or, for that matter, enlarging it from one scale to another is by photocopying. Most large towns have a photocopying bureau which, provided that plans are not being reduced or enlarged for commercial purposes, will be prepared to assist. The second method of enlarging and reducing – used before the advent of photocopiers, computer programmes and other aids to graphic art – is the square paper technique. If you wish to convert from ½ to half scale, place a piece of overhead projection film ruled in one-inch squares over your pattern, using Spray Mount or masking tape to secure it. Draw a grid of half inch squares on to plain paper and copy square by square from the master pattern.

So you want to make a project. Where do you start? Since I first started modelling in the late 1950s, the array of modelling materials, books on design and history, and other design materials has increased a thousandfold, at least. Most beginners start with a basic kit as their first project and you will find these described later in this book, together with the techniques which are necessary to customize and furnish them. Building from scratch is the only way to achieve truly unique models.

I have a noticeboard in my workroom on which I collect pictures, postcards, cuttings of material, scribbled drawings and anything else that may be useful for future projects. A very simple idea I picked up from knitting classes is a small colour sample. This consists of a piece of card sandwiched between two sheets of sandpaper. Round this is then wound ribbon or wool in colours which you wish to match, or try out to see if they go with each other. This small sample stick can then be carried round to enable you to buy bits and pieces for your room set in the way of fabric, paint or fittings and fixtures, and to be sure of matching textures and colours. When you design your room box it also helps to have a list of the furniture and fittings which you intend to include together with, even if this is only a magazine cutting, some idea of the sort of person who would live in your house.

Scratch-built projects are best tried out in rough. I make preliminary models out of cardboard, whether for houses or furniture. Having converted my drawing, or even just idea, into some sort of solid form, I usually move on to either wood or polyboard. You will find instructions on working these materials on pages 24–5 and 45. My Roman

Garden project is based on a series of historical novels by Lindsey Davis about one of the Emperor Vespasian's spies. As you can see, I have built a Roman garden. Falco and his beloved Helena are briefly free from wrestling with the family and the cooking pots and the rest of the human life that gave Falco so much trouble.

My sources for this were many and varied, but the ones that I found most useful were Lindsey Davis' books and the Usborne books on ancient history which are full of appropriate detail. For the beginner the advantage of this project is that it is a unique project but without particularly complicated furniture or clothing. For a professional teacher it would provide a useful exercise in social history. The basic structure can be applied to other centuries. It converts quite well to Norse and Tudor life as well as to more modern houses which you will see around you every day. I set out below how to get from the picture postcard to the finished model.

# DRAWING AND PLANS

In this section I describe the basic techniques for drawing plans and building models which have been used for hundreds of years. There are now many computerized drawing systems which can be used not only to prepare plans for building and for furniture, but also to enlarge and reduce drawings and to produce items such as brick paper and wallpaper by repeating images. In these days of relatively reasonably priced colour printers, it is not difficult to produce wallpaper and brick paper at home.

All buildings begin as plans, usually prepared by an architect. Once a building has been designed, plans are worked out and drawn accurately to scale. One of the best ways of understanding how plans are converted into models is to visit the Royal

Academy's summer exhibition. Although this is best known for pictures and sculpture, there is a section devoted to modern architecture which always contains beautiful architectural drawings, plans and models. It is a real joy for miniaturists and is often far more fulfilling than the larger works of art in the other, more important, rooms of the exhibition. Some people are lucky enough to be taught the neat, detailed drawing style used for plans at school, in technical drawing classes. Building plans are flat drawings of the three dimensional shape. Tools such as compasses, set squares and rulers make drawing arcs, angles and straight lines easier. Curves can be easily drawn by using a flexicurve or a set of French curves.

## DRAWING PLANS

There are three main steps to drawing a plan:

1. All measurements are worked out and a suitable scale is chosen, depending on the size of the desired building.
2. Information is gathered about all features required such as windows, walls, doors and even the position of fixtures such as stoves; work plans are then drawn.
3. The finished plan is drawn to scale using standard symbols for some features. Several elevations (sides) are usually shown.

There is, of course, nothing to stop you inventing a building or modelling your own home. You can also take a section out of a larger building – try doing just the tower of a castle.

## MAKING A ROUGH MODEL

Having drawn your plan and elevations, it is a good thing to try a rough model. For this, grocery boxes, cornflakes packets or

*¹⁄₁₂ scale shop exterior.*

any of the vast quantities of disposable packaging given away free can be used as a source of card. If you have difficulty in understanding the concept of plans and model making, then I recommend the purchase of one of the sets of cardboard villages from the suppliers listed at the back of this book, since these are a practical way of learning the art. You will need scissors, glue and tape; proceed as follows:

1. Lay out the building line. Put simply, this means drawing out the plan flat on your piece of card. Draw flaps down each open side for gluing together later.

2. Now draw details such as doors, windows and roof tiles. You could also paint in bricks, stones or tiles if you wish, or use stick-on paper.

3. Paint or colour the drawing, adding texture.

4. Cut the building out, fold and score the flaps, gluing the building together. It is sensible to reinforce the flaps with tape because of the amount of handling that working models receive. Paint a base on a piece of cardboard and glue your building to that.

Your next requirement is a shopping list.

# — 3 —

# Tools and Materials

## TOOLS

Listed here are the tools which I find most useful. For ease of reference, the section is in alphabetical order.

- Clamps. I hold models while I am working on them either with small G-clamps or bulldog clips or, if appropriate, with masking tape, rubber bands or elastic bands. Very small items can be held with children's modelling clay, Blu-Tack or grip wax. I also use a patented gadget called Helping Hands, and a small pin vice.
- Craft knives. I use both a Stanley knife with replaceable blades and also a range of modellers' knives. These are sold by model railway shops and specialist model suppliers. Change your blades frequently and always cut on a self-healing rubber mat or a cutting board.
- Dental equipment. This is useful for sculpting and is found at fairs and car boot sales.
- Drawing tools. As you will see throughout this book, I use a variety of drawing tools such as a set square, protractor and compass. Sets like this can even be obtained in supermarkets, especially at the beginning of the academic year.
- Drill. I use a mini electric drill with a selection of drill bits, sanding disks and cylindrical burrs.
- Jigs. A jig is any set-up which holds an assembly in a fixed position whilst the glue dries.

- Magnification. All but a lucky few people need to have some form of magnification. When working with small scales I use either a daylight bulb with an attached magnifying glass or a pair of magnifying lenses on a headband which fits over my usual spectacles.
- Mitre block. This is a block which enables right angles to be cut into beading and mouldings such as a skirting or picture framing. A small plastic one will do. You really cannot cut a true angle on a moulding without one. When mitring, make quite sure you know how the two pieces will fit together when cut, and be sure to lay the length on the correct side in the mitre block. Place the saw in the appropriate right- or left-angled slot and gently saw through. After a little trial and error, you'll soon get the hang of it.
- Pencils. I use a pencil both for marking wood and for tracing patterns. Use a sharp pencil for marking floorboards and a soft pencil for patterns.
- Pins. I use brass lace-making pins, glass-headed stainless steel pins and panel pins. A less-known use for glass-headed pins is as a modelling tool.
- Pliers. I have a selection of small pliers for bending wire and sheet metal. These can be obtained from hardware stores, jewellery suppliers or specialist suppliers. Also available from these sources are small wire cutters and tinsnips.
- Rubber bands. Use these for holding glued parts together whilst they dry.
- Sandpaper. Although it is tempting to use the coarsest grade, this can lead to distortion; it is better to use the finest

available grade of emery paper. I use a tack cloth to remove sanding dust and a small round or square file to finish work and to enlarge holes.

- Saw. I use a hacksaw and a junior fretsaw for cutting all sorts of wood. To cut MDF, always assuming I have not managed to persuade my friendly supplier, I use a power saw.
- Scissors. I have a large selection of specialist scissors. The ones I find most useful are a pair of découpage scissors. These are extremely sharp and have very small curved blades. I also have a pair of miniature scissors which have large handles. These are wonderful for getting into very small corners of fabric or paper. When sewing, I use embroidery scissors which have an integral curved stitch ripper. I cut almost everything with a pair of serrated all-purpose shears. These cut everything from carpet to thin metal and are sometimes called power scissors. Also useful are pinking shears and Friskas, which work in the same way as pinking shears but produce an elegant variety of patterns.
- Tweezers. A variety of tweezers is useful. You may find a pair with an integral magnifying glass is convenient for very small items.

There are two items of safety equipment which no modeller should be without. These are a dust mask and a pair of safety goggles, and can be obtained from DIY stores.

# ADHESIVES

It is essential to use the right adhesive not only so that it sticks properly, but also because the wrong adhesive may give off poisonous fumes or damage work. The most commonly used adhesive is white glue, sometimes referred to as PVA glue or tacky glue, which dries clear and can be used for most purposes. It is available in a number of thicknesses. Also useful are the following:

- Blu-Tack. This is a type of permanently pliant putty which is useful for temporary joining or to see how something is shaping up before gluing. It can leave a greasy mark on some wallpaper or fabric if used to hang pictures.
- Double-sided tape. Buy it from the hardware store in thick reels – this is more economical than buying it from the stationers. It is useful for sticking leather or thick fabric, such as miniature carpet, with no mess. It also allows for repositioning or replacing if you change your mind.
- Green modeller's putty. Invaluable for filling cracks and gaps, especially in white metal.
- Grip wax. Available from dolls' house suppliers, this allows such things as ornaments to stick to shelves or walls without looking obvious or causing damage in the form of staining.
- Milliput. This is a two-part putty which can be used for modelling, making moulds and also joining disparate items. Milliput, once dried, is very hard to remove.
- Spray Mount. This is pricey, but useful for hanging giftwrap wallpaper and for sticking some fabrics as it allows for repositioning. The bond becomes permanent over time. It must be used in a well-ventilated area.
- Superglue. This is useful for white metal and very small items. It can be used as either liquid or gel. Please read the instructions on the brand which you choose to use, particularly those relating to health and safety.
- Wood glue. Wood glue is essential for gluing wooden houses and furniture. It does take time to dry, but makes a strong bond. I use a hot-glue gun to 'tack' work together while the wood glue sticks.

# PAINTS

- Acrylic paints. These are fast drying and water-based paints. They do not usually need pre-mixing and brushes can be cleaned in water. They can be finished with clear varnish or lacquer applied by spray or brush.
- Oil paints. Oil-based paints sold by hobby ceramic suppliers are particularly good. These can be applied in a variety of ways and there is an ever-growing range of colours, although dark brown and black are the most useful. Many modellers use gold and silver solvent-based marker pens as an alternative to using a liner brush. Fibre-tipped pens now come in a variety of mediums. You can buy them for use with rubber stamps, with fabric and with china or glass.
- Spray paints. The best way to prime difficult surfaces, particularly resin, plastic and foam board, is to use car undercoat. This is available in dirty red, grey, white and black. It is the only way to make plastic user-friendly, and is useful for white metal. Do please remember that particularly white metal and resin blanks are often greasy and respond well to cleaning with hot water, detergent and a few drops of vinegar. Allow the piece to dry properly before painting.

# MODELLING COMPOUNDS AND CLAY

Much as I hate to state the obvious, there are a number of modelling materials which are unsuitable for use in a domestic setting, either because they are potentially toxic or because they present other health hazards. If you propose to use modelling clay and are a beginner, I recommend you start with a few lessons at a hobby ceramic studio to learn how to use the medium properly and the detailed safety precautions.

- Bread dough. This is popular for flowers and food.
- Cold porcelain. This is excellent for flowers and small-scale people.
- Epoxy putty. I use the best known brand, Milliput. It is a two-part epoxy putty which must be blended together. It has two uses: as a modelling compound or as a joining compound. It takes three hours to harden but the process can be speeded up with heat and small amounts will harden more quickly. Once hardened it has similar properties to Fimo. However, its useful adhesive properties allow it to bond. The regular sort is yellow grey in colour. Superfine white is useful for a porcelain effect and terracotta for earthenware. If you find Milliput too pliant to model with, leave it to harden for a while, then work quickly before it sets.
- Finishing materials. Many miniaturists use both spray starch and hard spray to arrange fabrics. As I find that both of these methods are affected by damp and do nothing for my asthma, I have an alternative method for treating fabric: I dip it in PVA medium.
- Modrock and other plaster bandages. These are useful for scenery and as formers.
- Papier mâché. This is another cheap and much maligned substance. There is a recipe on page 27. Its most obvious virtue is that it is cheap and strong. Furniture made out of papier mâché has been known to last for hundreds of years. It can be used for quite large structures, such as houses, as well as for small items like dolls and furniture. It is the material of choice for many railway modellers.
- Plasticine. This is the original children's modelling clay. It has much to recommend

it, not least the fact that it never goes truly hard. I use it to anchor plants and flowers in miniature landscapes and flower arrangements.

- Polyfilla. Many modellers already use this as a building material and apply it either neat or mixed with water and white glue to imitate stones or brickwork. It can also be used as a modelling material by saturating natural fibres with a solution and then allowing them to dry in the desired shape. This is used for scenery. The equivalent effect on clothes and soft furnishings can be achieved with 'Pretty Petal' or 'Stiffy'.

- Polymer clay. I use Fimo modelling material because at one time that was the only brand that was available, but other similar brands such as Sculpy and Formello are also available now. Fimo is very similar to the children's modelling compound, Plasticine, but it will harden permanently when baked in a conventional oven. Sue Heaser is the leading authority on working with this medium; her books appear in the Bibliography.

- Salt dough. This is a dough which can be made from flour, salt and water, sometimes with other ingredients added. This is one of the oldest modelling substances and can be used not only for miniatures' bread but for a whole range of figures, furniture and accessories. It keeps surprisingly well if it is properly varnished.

- Transfer medium. There are a number of these products available, particularly from hobby supermarkets. They can be used to convert paper and material into transfers, which is a useful skill. A transfer medium from Dylon can be used to transfer print to fabric; it is called Image Maker and seems to work best with coloured photocopies and smooth fabrics such as cotton. Art shops sell other transfer media.

# STAINS AND VARNISHES

- Varnish. The range of varnishes available is huge. I prefer to use clear acrylic varnish which can be obtained in gloss, matt, semi-matt and pearl finishes. Many modellers use traditional French polish, and nail varnish has its uses. Most polymeric clays have their own varnish which you should use for projects with this medium. The wrong varnish can discolour or damage your work. In small scales it is more effective to spray a coat of primer on a piece of work which you wish to customize than to use varnish stripper. If you do wish to use varnish stripper, use it according to the instructions and wear protective clothes and goggles. Furniture polish can be used to finish items. I also use pre-coloured shoe polish on both wood and cardboard.

- Wood stain. Wood stain can be water- or spirit-based. It comes in a huge variety of colours and can be diluted. It is worth remembering to test the desired colour first. Please remember that most stains do not take over glue. Stain your piece in its unassembled form and then glue it.

# KIT BUILDING

If you begin your career as a modeller by making a few kit houses, particularly if they are made in different scales, you will become used to the materials needed to complete a project. Kits vary according to price as to what they contain. House kits from reputable suppliers such as the Dolls House Emporium, will contain pre-cut wooden shapes for the basic structure, windows including the clear plastic necessary to glaze the windows, staircase parts, turnings for the staircase rails and interior and exterior doors. Sometimes they will contain other fittings, such as architectural mouldings. Kits may also contain fabrics, white metal parts or hardware necessary to complete the basic model. It is unusual for kits to contain wallpaper and paint, since these are so much a question of personal taste. Even if you are completing a kit from a well-known and reputable supplier, it is still sensible to read through the directions and parts list. Check that all the parts referred to have been included in the kit and that there are no additional items that you need to purchase and install in the course of completing the kit.

# SCRATCH BUILDING

## FOUND AND RECYCLED MATERIALS

If you scratch build, you will be using most probably one or more of the found or recycled materials described below.

I cannot recommend too highly the habit of saving small scraps and pieces from all sorts of sources as all kinds of oddments can come in handy. Most kits will yield bits and pieces of waste wood, if nothing else, or plastic or even spare items which you do not need. Even white-metal castings yield remnants which can be used in future projects; keep them in a filing system. Lifelong modellers often have a system for filing parts for future use. My husband's is based on plastic ice-cream boxes which are numbered and indexed

Preliminary models can be made from packaging, as I mentioned above, or from the grey board at the back of notebooks and sketch pads. This cardboard is also extremely useful for building furniture. You should always keep thin pieces of wood: they can be found from orange boxes, fruit and vegetable punnets, and the sort of wooden box in which some glacé fruit is sold. It is also always worth looking

through the remnants box at DIY shops and hardware stores.

Chocolate boxes and other food packages yield, as well as useful printed material and cardboard, glazing material in various thicknesses. Bigger packages contain polystyrene and various sorts of plastic sheet. Takeaway Chinese meals produce mirror glass in the lids, and foil which can be cut up for flashing, roofing, armour and so on. There are innumerable plastic containers which lend themselves to use as building components. The Egyptian Temple on page 116 and the Roman Garden on page 154 both started as scrap. A word of caution, however: it is a good idea to check what sort of glue you need to stick particular packaging or metal; your local model shop will be able to assist if you are in doubt.

### Cardboard or Matt Board
Artists' supply shops and stationers should be a first port of call. Picture mounting board, sometimes called matt board, is white on one side and coloured on the other. It comes in a range of colours because it is intended to set off the picture it is used to frame. It can be bought in sheets from art suppliers, but it would be sensible for modellers to check the remnants box. These will have already been cut with a bevelled edge at an angle of 45 degrees, which means that they can be stuck together as part of small-scale buildings. Almost any colour will do, since it will be covered with whatever your finish will be. Artist mounting board in the usually available thickness of 1.5mm (1/16in) is appropriate to small-scale buildings in quarter scale and below. It bends too easily to be used without support in larger projects, but can be laminated for use in furniture. Cardboard does absorb moisture from the atmosphere and will, therefore, warp over time. This can be prevented by coating it with varnish. It can also be used

*Cars and motor bikes (half scale).*

as cladding or tiling in larger scales (*see* the Dress Shop on page 18)

*Plastic Sheet*
Many modellers use plastic sheet, sometimes called styrene sheet, which is sold under a number of brand names. This looks like postcard and is available in a variety of colours and thicknesses. It is clean to work with, easy to cut, sand and file, and can be easily painted. It is much loved for railway, machinery and road vehicle modelling since it is much easier to work than metal. Also available, and very useful for small-scale furniture, is a variety of plastic strips, tubes and pre-formed windows, doors and building finishes. Suitable solvents can be obtained and these dry very quickly. The same solvents, incidentally, can often be used for proprietary furniture kits from firms like Chrysnbon. There is also a large range of kits in this material

predominantly aimed at the model railway-building fraternity. These are easy to convert to miniature houses, as can be seen from the garage on page 166 and the Double 'O' scale complex on page 164. Commercially available embossed styrene sheet is obtainable in the following finishes: brick, stone, corrugated iron, clap boarding, metal, slate, tiles and even drystone walling.

Styrene and Plasticard can be obtained from most model shops or by mail order. It is also the best material for making modern kitchen appliances such as sink units and fridges. Larger structures will need support. Printed paper cut-outs for modern appliances are available at fairs in $\frac{1}{12}$ and half scale.

*Wood*
There is a school of thought that assumes that the best modelling material for any

item is that in which it would have been made in full scale. This is just workable in $\frac{1}{2}$ scale, except that bricks tend to become increasingly fragile the smaller they get and stone is pretty heavy. I deal with brick and stone finishing materials below. Wood is the most commonly used material for dolls' house building. Both plywood and the ubiquitous MDF are used. MDF stands for Medium-Density Fibreboard. Both can be easily cut with power tools in particular, and you will see in the Bibliography that I have recommended a number of books on making wooden dolls' houses; plans and basic shell kits may be obtained from the suppliers given in the List of Suppliers. Plans are often given away free in dolls' house magazines.

Both MDF and plywood have disadvantages for the amateur modeller. Plywood, for instance, warps easily. What beginner has not at some stage been frustrated by a kit which has been in store too long and now does not fit together because it is warped? MDF has a nasty habit of spreading dust when cut, and dust is a health hazard. For these reasons, work in a well-ventilated workshop with a dust extractor and face mask or, alternatively, work out of doors with a face mask, observing in either case any instructions the manufacturer of your tools may have given about safety. Plywood or MDF shells can be put together with butt joints or angle joints using pins and white glue; use white glue sold specifically for woodwork.

There are a number of specialist wood suppliers who cater for house-modellers both amateur and professional. Particularly in furniture, wood, particularly well-chosen hardwood, makes for high quality work.

## Foam Board
Foam board, sometimes called foam core, is more costly than wood. Particularly for female modellers who may be intimidated

by the paraphernalia needed to make models in wood, the number of tools, the expense of power tools and the supposed strength needed to work in wood, foam core is an ideal solution. The board can be joined with ordinary tacky glue on butt joints using pins, preferably brass ones or the glass-headed stainless steel ones, to hold the pieces while the glue sets, which is a matter of minutes. Marking out the model can be done easily on the white surface and cutting requires no very great strength or skill, providing a sharp blade is used. The board can be laminated to give greater strength in larger scales. Any tendency to warp can be prevented by coating both the exterior and the interior with diluted white glue. Modelling clay and Polyfilla can be used as finishing materials as can Plasticard, card and proprietary bricks and tiles. Foam board is particularly suitable for half-scale and quarter-scale buildings.

## Polystyrene
Anyone who has ever bought white goods such as washing machines will have received huge quantities of thick white polystyrene. This is useful for test models and for supporting landscaping in both larger and smaller scales. It is also easy to carve. Proprietary hot wire carvers can be bought from craft suppliers. The product can be painted and finished in a variety of ways, as can be seen from the chapters on landscaping and gardening. Polystyrene is useful for landscaping but not suitable for elaborate structural use. Some adhesives will dissolve it: tacky glue is probably the most acceptable.

## Clay
I learnt to model in clay at school. It was not until I had completed my university course and done evening classes in pottery that I realized there was a relatively simple and satisfactory way of building houses and

a number of the accessories to go in them: from the same sort of clay that is used for production line dinnerware and, indeed, bathroom fittings in full size. This liquid clay, usually called 'slip', is cast in commercially produced moulds made from plaster of Paris. The water from the clay poured into the mould is absorbed into the plaster and it is then possible to turn out the rigid unfired, 'greenware', shape. Once this is dried a little further it can be trimmed and tidied up with a number of tools including ordinary household scourers and sponges. The resulting shape can then be fired for the first time, when it becomes biscuit or bisque ware, and then painted or glazed. If glazed, the work must then be fired again.

It is possible to imitate most of the major ceramic products in common use, particularly dinnerware and otherwise expensive items such as floor tiles, by using products sold for the hobby ceramics market. You do not need to own a kiln: there are many studios around the country providing a firing service. Usually these also provide comprehensive lessons and the products necessary to make your project. It is even possible within the limitations of clay to make quite large houses. My column in *Dolls House and Miniature Scene* featured the Hallowe'en project shown on page 86 and known as Count Dracula's Country Cottage. The original mould for this project is a commercial mould made by the American company Ceramichrome.

There are a number of other clay items which make suitable houses. I have also featured in my column a pottery village which is based on vegetable shapes. There are several pumpkins, gourds and a mushroom shown in the accompanying photograph. The inhabitants are small mice and they have a playground made up of various sorts of fruit – there is even a radish bandstand! A step-by-step guide to making and painting the pumpkin and a shopping list for necessary supplies appears on page 84.

Making bricks and tiles requires different sorts of clay. On the whole, for brickwork I would recommend the air-hardening clay sold under the brand name 'Das' because of its ease of use. Alternatively, real bricks can be bought. Floor tiles and bathroom tiles are a different matter: they exist in a limited range and can also be made from Plasticard or from various polymer clays. However, if you wish to have the quality of real tiles and the full colour range, then there is nothing to beat cutting out small squares of clay, painting them with proprietary hobby ceramic colours, bisque firing and then glazing them with clear glaze, and then firing them again. These are particularly attractive for conservatories, kitchens, bathrooms and hallways. These tiles can be easily cut with a tile cutter; mosaic tiles can also be used.

Another alternative to making tiles in a mould is to roll out white earthenware and paint it with hobby ceramic products. To obtain this earthenware you will have to visit a potters' supply shop. A quarter bag and a tessarae cutter will, however, provide you with a huge number of tiles. You may also feel like making yourself a few dolls' house dolls. Suppliers of bathroom suite moulds, food, dinnerware and doll moulds are given at the back of the book.

Another useful structural building material is papier mâché: two recipes for it are on pages 27 and 28. This is an extremely cheap, readily accessible material and it should not be assumed that it is only suitable for children. Anyone who has admired the works of Penny Thompson will know it is possible to achieve truly masterly representations of English vernacular buildings, if you have the necessary skills.

## FINISHING MATERIALS

Even the relatively short space of time encompassed by my husband's and my joint modelling careers has seen a huge increase in the number of finishing materials available other than paint, varnish and traditional woodwork finishes. For example, oil marker pens and metallic wax can be used to give truly splendid finishes for both buildings and furniture, and gold and other metal leaves can be obtained from artist suppliers and are now relatively cheap. These can be applied over a painted item on to a coat of size or glue.

Some items which do not seem immediately useful to modellers can be obtained. There is a wide range of shoe polishes and shoe dyes which are useful for furniture and for 'dirtying-up' various buildings to give them the patina of age. I have used a number of natural materials to finish projects, such as seeds and shells. These need to be substantially varnished to preserve them. I have also used a variety of items for thatch. These include plaster of Paris, Das, Isopon, string, railway modellers' vegetation and coir materials. Plaster of Paris and Das both make satisfactory roofing materials. Asthmatics should note, though, that coir and Isopon can cause difficulties.

## OTHER USEFUL SUPPLIERS

There are a variety of other suppliers who sell – in some cases inadvertently – items which are of use to the modeller. Jewellery findings and egg-craft products are useful, particularly the small metal findings. Cake decorating shops sell wonderful non-stick rollers and boards as well as a range of moulds and the ever-useful cold porcelain which actually shrinks substantially, making it very suitable for architectural mouldings in smaller scales. Model railway shops and model shops generally, particularly those that specialize in military modelling, war games and mechanical models, have a range of components which may be useful. I have found those shops which specialize in model boats particularly useful because their small wooden turnings are beautifully made and can be used for so many different

purposes. Apart from using bits of material from other miniature disciplines, a model car or boat can add charm and authenticity to a house. (*See* the photographs on page 28.)

## PAPIER MÂCHÉ

There are two main ways of using papier mâché to model with: as pulp or as layers of paper glued together, used to cover existing objects. Papier mâché may be used for covering cardboard former-shapes for free modelling, and for moulding.

*Materials*
• Old newspapers or proprietary dehydrated pulp
• Wheat or wallpaper paste such as Polycell
• Dilute 50/50 white glue

*Covering a Pre-existing Shape*
This is the best way for beginners to start. You will need a shape that is structurally sound, such as a strong cardboard box. Remember that the article you choose will remain inside the coating of papier mâché. There is no reason why, if making a house, you should not model the interior as well. Your box should be clean and grease free. You can use old newspaper, kitchen paper, tissue or sugar paper which gives a pleasantly textured effect. Paper can be torn up into strips or squares, or cut into triangles. If you want the finished effect to be a smooth one, then tearing is best. If you wish to give the impression of bricks or stone, then cut the edges of the paper appropriately into similarly sized shapes. Either dip the strips or squares of paper into a bowl of paste and force out the excess paste in your fingers, or paint the glue directly on to the paper with a brush. You can then apply the paper to your former. If working over a card box you will usually need at least three layers.

*Boats (⅟₁₂ scale).*

Start along one side and work in rows as if laying bricks.

Once your object has been completely covered with three or more layers of papier mâché, you should leave it to dry. Depending on the weather and how warm your house is, this will take between one and three days. Once it is completely dry you must seal your work: this can be done with white tacky glue diluted half and half with water. Glue dries transparent so you may wish to consider mixing your PVA glue with artists' acrylic colour, or using an emulsion paint.

Structural details and decoration can be built into the papier mâché with additional paper either cut or moulded into the shapes you require, such as wall panelling, and glued on when dry. You can make use of found objects such as string, lace, seeds, textured paper, paper doilies, strip wood and fabric. Needless to say, papier mâché provides an excellent basis for paint.

The other alternative is papier mâché pulp, made by soaking torn-up newspaper in warm water. It is sensible to start with at least ten to fifteen newspapers torn up – tearing is preferable to cutting since it breaks down the fibres more effectively and is quicker. Leaving the paper in warm water overnight is useful. The next morning you can pulp it with a stick, take out handfuls of pulp, squeeze it to remove water, and then leave it in lumps on a surface such as a piece of plywood. There are two important things to remember when modelling with pulp. Firstly, never, ever tip the sludge down a drain or sink as it can block up the plumbing most effectively. Secondly, there is no point in washing your

hands midway in the production of pulp. All that this does is to remove the natural oils on your hands, which form a barrier to printer's ink, and ensure that the second lot of hand washing is much less effective than the first.

Break up your damp pulp into crumbs and either sprinkle dry wallpaper paste on to it or add diluted white glue, until you have a slippery modelling paste. If you are making figures you may require very fine papier mâché and this can be best achieved by putting the papier mâché and glue in a old electric blender in small quantities. This allows for fine detail such as faces.

To cover an existing simple form such as a bowl, it is easiest to use cling wrap or foil. You could use vaseline as an alternative mould release, but it is messy and almost impossible to get rid of the grease to allow for a satisfactory painted finish. This method needs a former without any undercuts. In other words you need to use a shape where the papier mâché comes off the mould more easily. Tear old newspapers up and dip them into a bowl of Polycell, removing excess glue with your fingers, then lay the strips over the mould. Cover the entire mould and then cover it with three or four layers. Make sure that there are no air bubbles. Before the papier mâché is dry you should trim it with a pair of scissors. Combinations of articles may be used to make a house.

If you wish to use a mould which is undercut, you should cover the former with foil or plastic wrap and then follow the steps above. Once the papier mâché is dry, cut it in half down one side across the bottom and up the other side. The paper shell will then come off the mould quite easily. You will then need to tape the two halves together with masking tape and then cover the join with two or three layers of glued paper strips. Papier mâché can be used both for houses and for making small people and furniture – *see* left and page 91.

*Papier mâché house form (HobbyCraft).*

# 4

# Making Miniature People and Animals

The world of dolls' house miniaturists is pretty well divided into those who like to have occupants for their houses and those who feel that occupants other than perhaps the occasional cat or dog detract from the overall effect. Whatever scale you usually model in, dolls can present something of a problem in a dolls' house. Valuable antique dolls' houses are often occupied by a large family of children, mother, father and an enviable retinue of servants and nursemaids who either stand solemnly to attention, lie in a dead faint or spend their entire lives staring at the ceiling. This is a particular problem with porcelain dolls. Even the most beautiful porcelain dolls today are not easy to play with and, particularly in half scale and downwards, will not sit, stand, bend or lie in anything that resembles a natural position.

Some years ago I went to a course on making sugar flowers at my local technical college in the hope that this would improve my modelling skills, particularly for Fimo flowers, fruit and vegetables. My cake-icing friends all raved about sugar paste and flower paste as modelling mediums. They are quite right. Unfortunately, these excellent mediums don't last forever and are irresistible to mice, small children, and so on. Sometime later I was given a sample of cold porcelain together with some magazines in Spanish and sometime after that a video on making flowers. The cold porcelain was excellent, the video was terrific, but I found it very difficult to obtain further supplies of the medium or the bits and pieces needed to work with cold porcelain. Even flower cutters, which were described as very small, tended to be too large even for $\frac{1}{2}$ scale. I kept on asking everyone I met, both in the craft and cake icing world and eventually discovered that Cel Craft were importing an improved version of A si es cold porcelain paste and supplying cutters, modelling tools and so on. Just before I was driven to Spanish evening classes, an English version of the videos and a number of excellent books were also produced.

For those of you who are even newer to this excellent modelling material, there is even a group called the Porcelain Society who publish a quarterly newsletter with lots of hints, tips and projects. The address of their Membership Secretary is Alan Dunn, 222 Prince Consort Road, Gateshead, Tyne and Wear NE8 4DX.

Cold porcelain paste is made up from a mixture of glue, preservatives and cornflour with oil sometimes added. There are a number of recipes given in *Modelling and Cold Porcelain* by Tombi Peck and Alan Dunn. If you want to make your own cold porcelain then the recipes in this book are a good place to start. It should be noted that the most commonly used preservative, sodium benzoate, together with the dust involved in the raw ingredients, is not ideal for asthmatics. The commercially made pastes are readily available by mail order and from craft suppliers. My favourite is the original A si es paste imported from Argentina where it was originally developed. I found this an extremely satisfactory modelling material both for the projects listed in the books supplied and for making items such as plates, cups and saucers and so on.

Whether you work in cold porcelain or in some other modelling medium, there are moulds available for fruit, vegetables, figures, flowers, birds, teddy bears, mice, rabbits and the sort of decorative features which can be adapted for dolls' house architectural fittings. Cold porcelain has a lot to recommend it as a medium for elaborate plaster ceilings: motifs can be repeated easily and are much less fragile than plaster of Paris.

There are similarities between sugar craft, Fimo and cold porcelain techniques. However, there are some basic rules which beginners in particular need to follow to ensure success. Whichever brand of paste you use, it will need to be kept in an airtight container. Commercial paste is supplied in double-wrapped packs which require very little kneading. If the paste sticks to your fingers, use a cold cream such as Nivea (just a tiny amount) when kneading. Do not add too much. The experts are right when they say that this toughens the paste. If your paste becomes too tough to work, add a very little warm water drop by drop. Lubricate tools and work boards with a small amount of cold cream, removing most of it before rolling out the cold porcelain. Cornflour can be used to stop the paste from sticking, particularly if you are using a leaf veiner or fine cutters.

Cold porcelain can be coloured for working by the addition of small quantities of designers' gouache. The experts recommend that a small quantity of permanent white gouache is added to the paste to reduce its translucency. Other colours can be used; it is essential to remember that the colour becomes darker as it dries. To add petals to a flower or more porcelain to a model figure use tacky glue, which can be diluted. Either paint on to the model with a brush or pipe through a glue dispenser.

Water can be used to moisten models, to smooth them and also to lubricate tools.

There is an enormous range of paints and colours which can be used to colour models. Artists' oils and acrylics as well as watercolour can be used either separately or in conjunction. I also use craft dust, available from Cel Craft. These are tiny pots of pure pigment which can be dusted on delicately or mixed with a carrying medium such as white spirit or an acrylic medium such as Modge Podge.

From the point of view of a dedicated half-scaler-and-down modeller, I found Holly Product's book on clowns extremely useful. It would be wrong to say that modelling half-scale and quarter-scale figures from scratch is easier than modelling in $\frac{1}{12}$ scale. Any product or tool which widens the scope for half scalers has to be good news. As a rough guide, anything described in a cold porcelain or sugar paste supplier's catalogue as 'fairy' will usually convert without too much difficulty into a half scale figure. For those of you who are profoundly tired of half scale models which cannot be posed, this could prove to be the answer.

The best way to start learning about cold porcelain modelling is to attend a class. If you are not able to do this, there are videos and books available that may be of use. Cel Craft produce two videos, one on flowers and the other on figures. As far as books go, *Cold Porcelain Projects* by Margaret Ford contains all the basic techniques, a number of beginners' projects such as brooches, earrings and fridge magnets, a section on flowers and pot plants (full scale), a section on miniatures, a section on modelling, and more advanced projects.

Tombi Peck and Alan Dunn's book referred to above contains flowers so real they are breathtaking. The miniatures include bonsai, miniature roses, a caladium, a mother-in-law's tongue, daffodils and tulips, a camellia arrangement and a fern. For half scalers and frustrated doll makers who are struggling with figure modelling, the book which I really recommend is June Twelve's book on clowns. The clowns are gorgeous, but the figure-making instructions and the face moulds could be applied through all the common miniaturist's scales of $\frac{1}{12}$, half and quarter scale. June's firm, Holly Products, sell a wide range of moulds to help with figure making and also patterns to be used with modelling paste. They also sell embossing tools and texturing tools which will be of use to modellers (*see* the furniture in the Half Scale Hotel on page 67).

Half scale people are not as readily available in dolls' house shops as $\frac{1}{12}$ scale, but there is a simple way of making small figures.

These figures can have clothes moulded on to them. You will see from the picture below, I made a landlord and customers for my half-timbered public house from Sue and Alan's Little Treasures. These figures and their clothes are made from cold porcelain.

*Materials*

- Cold porcelain
- Cel Craft's fairy moulds
- Small curved pointed scissors
- Craft knife
- Cel Pad
- Cocktail sticks
- Soft foam or bubble pack (to work on)

*Interior, Tudor public house.*

The fairy moulds come in two large sheets which are marked with a letter of the alphabet so that the two halves of each mould can be paired. Cut along the marked line to make up matching pairs of limbs and body parts. It is not a good idea to use the same set of moulds for sugar craft and for cold porcelain. When working cold porcelain paste use a little Nivea or cold cream both on your hands and on working surfaces. The cold cream can also be used as a mould release agent: coat the moulds with a very little cold cream and wipe back any surplus with tissue.

*Body, Arms and Legs*

Body and limbs should be made from paste coloured with flesh-coloured designer's gouache. I find that three pea-size blobs are enough to tint one of the heart-shaped packages in a pack of cold porcelain. Remember that colours darken as they dry. The method is as follows:

1. Roll the paste into a sausage shape approximately the size and shape of the mould.
2. Clip the mould sides together and place the paste into one half of a matching pair of moulds, making sure that the studs interlock; you may need to adjust the size of your piece of paste to begin with.
3. Squeeze the mould together, then open it and carefully trim away any excess paste with a craft knife, taking care not to cut the plastic mould.
4. Close the mould and squeeze it again.
5. Trim again and remove the leg, arm or body from the mould.
6. Smooth any rough edges with a modelling tool and water.

This is the time to adjust your figure. For example, legs may need to be bent to fit a particular chair or hand-crafted to hold a toy or a cup. I usually make a selection of figures, having decided on the general theme, in this case a rather riotous evening at the pub. Pinch the top of the legs and arms slightly so that they can be stuck to the body easily.

*The Face*

When the selected body piece has dried completely, take a small ball of flesh-coloured paste and press it into one of the face moulds. Skim away any excess paste, level to the mould surface. Coat the flat head back with white glue (such as Aileen's Tacky Glue or Modge Podge) and press on to the soft paste whilst still in the body mould. Lift away and the face will be attached. Smooth paste over the hard head to neaten the join. When dry, about a day in good weather, facial details can be painted on with a very fine brush or the tip of a cocktail stick.

Hair styles can be achieved in a number of ways. A smocking tool from Holly Products can be used to make a smooth French pleat or bun style, or for a pageboy. The same tool can be used for short, flapper-style haircuts and is particularly useful for men's hair. Curly styles and ringlets are best achieved by pushing the paste through a garlic press. Ringlets can be made somewhat laboriously by winding the resulting strips of paste round a cocktail stick. Short curls can be made from shorter strands or by unravelling Bunka braid or lampshade trim.

Figures can be assembled at the dressing stage. If making a female figure in a long frock, there is no need to make separate legs and feet. Simply carve a piece of Cel Block or dry flower oasis roughly into shape or, alternatively, crumple up a piece of tinfoil.

The sequence for making body pieces and assembly is as follows:

1. Make moulded body, arms and legs and dry thoroughly.
2. Place socks and boots on the legs before fixing to body.
3. Fill joints if required.
4. Make and position skirt, trousers or shorts.

5. Make blouse, jacket or other top and place on the upper body.
6. Make collar and other trimmings and add a suitable long hair style (if required).
7. Make sleeves and add to the arms before fixing in place on the body.
8. Add hat or hair trimmings and make suitable props.
9. When completely dry, paint in additional detail.
10. Add non-paste trimmings.

Unlike Fimo or sugar paste, cold porcelain does not stick to itself. Each piece has to be glued and it is, therefore, sensible to use a glue bottle of white glue. You may find, particularly in hot weather, that glue needs to be diluted. Do not use the thicker decorator's glue as this tends to clump.

Now to the clothes for individual figures. The two peasant girls/tavern wenches on page 163 are made in much the same way, save that one is seated and the other is standing. The pattern pieces for their dresses have been textured with a smocking tool. Their shawls and cream-coloured aprons have been frilled by rolling a cocktail stick or frilling tool backwards and forwards along the paste before it is applied. The hair styles are shown in the diagram. The frilled cap is made by pinching out a small ball of paste into a flat circle and then forming it over a tiny oval of scrunched up tinfoil.

The yokel with a beard sitting on the settle with his arm round one of the wenches has simple tubes of paste as trousers and a smock made with a piece of smocking constructed by using a smocking tool and pinching the stripes of smocking with a pair of tweezers as shown in the diagram supplied with the smocking tool. The other seated yokel, probably the landlord, is made in the same way, save that he has a long waistcoat cut from paste and a scarf round his neck.

The last two figures are intended to be a highwayman and his female companion, on page 162. These were dressed in clothes taken from a reproduction of a Hogarth print. I pre-coloured the paste for the highwayman's coat using four pea-size dots of cobalt black paint in a half block of paste. This left me with enough to make breeches and shoes as well. The coat has been decorated by using a mini-embossing stick from Holly Products with a pattern of leaves and strawberries. The breeches are rectangles which have been textured with a smocking tool. I dry-brushed the breeches with white and highlighted the embossed pattern with gold and copper paint. The arrangement for the powdered wig is basically textured blobs. It is quite sufficient to make just three or four ringlets. If you want the effect of a powdered wig, use black paste and dry-brush it several times with white acrylic.

I use a variety of paints and small trimmings to add character to my cold porcelain figures. Pearlized paint looks like satin or silk if applied over paste of the same colour. Thus green pearlized paint (which looks white in the tubes) should be applied over mid- to dark-green paste. Glitter glue can be used as jewels if dotted on with a pin or cocktail stick. Gilding wax is available in many colours besides the usual gold, silver and copper. I use Liberon 'Saint-Germain' and 'Rambouillet' both separately and mixed together to give the effect of battered armour when used over dark grey or black paste. Both Bunka trimming and sections of lace can also be used. Sections of lampshade braid and dolls' house furniture prints can be cut down to make them suitable for half scale models. I also use metallic crochet cotton and embroidery floss. Egg-craft suppliers also sell a big range of tiny beads, rhinestones and filigrees.

Finally, a word about copyright. This method of making dolls enables you to make small figures quite quickly. None of the moulds or patterns referred to above should be used other than for private consumption. For commercial use you must obtain the permission of the copyright owner of a mould

# Tips and Problem-Solving

- Cold porcelain shrinks. Adverse effects can be avoided by allowing body parts to dry before assembling them. Cracks can be filled by making a paste from cold porcelain of the same colour and water, and using this in much the same way as Polyfilla. Remember, though, that a little extra glue may be necessary. Large cracks, particularly in clothes, should be filled by painting over the gap with tacky glue before adding paste.

- Standing figures, particularly in larger scales, will need an armature. Use florists' wires, cocktail sticks, cake icing wire or rolled silver foil. Whichever you choose will need to be covered with glue before cold porcelain is applied to it. Large-scale heads need to be filled with a cotton ball. These are not sold in small enough sizes for half scale figures but you can save paste by using silver paper as a filler. Occasionally your model may crack over an armature; the crack can be repaired with paste or perhaps the foil painted to match the figure.

- Skirted figures may need to have a circle of paper or fabric glued over the base to conceal Cel Block or silver foil used to support a skirt.

- It is helpful to make figures with a rather smaller waist than usual. Remember that female figures may need padding to achieve suitable line. For the right physical shape, refer to a costume book.

- Coloured porcelain darkens as it dries. To lighten the colour, dry-brush with a flat hogs-hair brush and a lighter shade of the same colour. This technique is particularly useful when salvaging flesh-coloured paint which has become too dark as it has dried.

- If your figure will not stand properly, consider gluing it to a small plaque of cold porcelain or providing it with a cloak or a strategically placed extension to existing clothing. Some accessories can also be used to achieve stability; a shepherd's crook or a golf club, for example.

- Figures which will be subjected to a lot of handling should be varnished for protection. Gloss varnish repels fingerprints best, although matt looks more satisfactory on flesh and fabric.

- With small children or babies, there is no need to model the complete body. Simply make hands, feet and a head and arrange clothes suitably around them.

- Sugar paste users, who will probably have graduated from cake decorating classes, often ask whether dusting colours can be used. As a general rule, the edible dusting colours fade quite quickly and it is, therefore, more sensible to use craft dust, whose pigments are stronger. These do need to be applied to damp work: if your work has dried out, wipe it over with a baby wipe. If all else fails, craft dust can be added to media, such as Modge Podge, to make quite a satisfactory combined paint and varnish. Most art shops sell PVA medium which can also be used in this way.

*(continued overleaf)*

# *Tips and Problem-Solving* (continued)

- There is a whole gallery of modelling tools sold by cake suppliers and art suppliers. Do not forget that there is also a wide variety of household items which can be used as satisfactory modelling tools, including cocktail sticks, barbecue sticks, stamp tweezers, small knives, blunt pencils, pen tops, old biros, wool needles and old toothbrushes. Some of these can be made more satisfactory by carving or shaping them in some way. Embossing tools are most useful, but you will often find that a piece of packaging has a satisfactory texture. Two examples are a rose pattern from a bottle of shampoo of the sort supplied by hotels in miniature sizes, and various pan scourers which make a quilted or tile texture if rolled into modelling paste.

- My personal experience of Polymer clay, which is plastic based, is that it sticks to plastic moulds. If you wish to make figures along the lines of those described above from Fimo or Sculpy, then you will have to trace a source of solid resin moulds which are specifically described as being suitable for polymer clay. Many hobby supermarkets and mail order hobby suppliers carry suitable moulds. Their scale, however, needs to be checked very carefully.

- If your cold porcelain has become too hard, it can be softened by the addition of a few drops of water. If it is too soft, simply leave the block of paste unwrapped in a dry atmosphere.

- When using foam as an armature, use either Cel Block, available from Cel Crafts, or the grey oasis intended for dried flowers. Neither green oasis, which tends to colour the paste, nor commercial polystyrene, are suitable.

- There are a number of small accessories which can be easily made from cold porcelain either to use with a figure or as stand-alone items for a shop. These include hats for both sexes, underwear, stockings, gloves, aprons, pinafores, corsets, night clothes and dresses. If making a row of dresses to hang up in a shop, bear in mind that these will look more authentic if they are moulded over a few folds of tinfoil or a small piece of bubble wrap. The most satisfactory method of making hats from cold porcelain is to use the blisters from a pack of pills or cough sweets.

- There are three books which I recommend to modellers. The first is *The Little People* by Margaret Ford and obtainable from Cel Cakes and cake icing shops, and the others are *Mad about Clowns* and *Making Babies* from Holly Products.

before selling your work. Copyright law and, indeed, all intellectual property is a detailed legal topic. If you plan to sell your work you should seek the advice of a solicitor if you wish either to protect your own original artwork or if you wish to use moulds, patterns or drawings created by someone else.

## METAL FIGURES

Collecting and painting model soldiers has a long and honourable history. For those who are unable or do not have enough confidence to make their own figures, this offers a simple and satisfying way of producing figures and scenes with little more effort than is required, as one manufacturer says, 'to assemble a simple plastic kit or paint a children's colouring book'. As with any other hobby there are a number of magazines, clubs and shows devoted to the hobby. Figures are available in a variety of scales of which $\frac{1}{32}$ or 54mm, half or 75mm and $\frac{1}{12}$ or 130mm are the commonest and most useful to dolls' house modellers.

These white-metal castings are extremely detailed. They are relatively cheap and can be used in conjunction with proprietary white-metal furniture which is historically accurate and of a very high standard. In particular, the white-metal range of male figures complement porcelain female figures well, since male clothing, and particularly uniforms, is difficult to produce in small scales from cloth or paper. Many of the white metal castings available are produced by internationally known sculptors and are, therefore, of a very high quality.

These figures are particularly useful for large scenes and dioramas. The majority of dolls' houses do not contain sufficient room for a ballroom scene if $\frac{1}{12}$ scale is used. In $\frac{1}{32}$ scale, a ball or assembly is perfectly possible and much more reasonably priced. Similar considerations apply to period seaside scenes. Metal figures are also cheaper than porcelain and come in a wide range of periods, ages and characters.

### Typical Assembly

A typical white-metal kit comprises all the component parts needed to assemble the basic model. Most kits are produced in white-metal alloy which faithfully reproduces all the fine detail of the original model. Some kits may include brass etched parts or components of a different material, for reasons of manufacture or for their suitability of the purpose. For example, more delicate items may be stronger if etched in brass. It is possible to add more accessories to the basic model or by grouping or mounting figures to expand a diorama or miniature scene. More experienced modellers may modify the figure to create individual items or to add variation to a theme.

### What You Need to Build the Models

The manufacturers tend to supply detailed instructions. As a general rule you will require the following cheap, basic tools:

- Half round needle file
- Full round needle file
- Craft knife
- Hardboard or plywood building board or self-healing board
- Small quantity of plasticine or Blu-Tack, to support models
- Fine 'wet and dry' emery paper
- Metal adhesive (quick set epoxy cement, for example)
- Toothpicks or cocktail sticks are useful for mixing and applying adhesive

Your local model or craft shop should help you with supplies of the above. For painting figures you will require good quality paint brushes in at least sizes 0 and 00.

### Assembly and Painting

You will typically have to start by cleaning up the parts to remove joint lines or feed marks. White metal is relatively soft and this can be done with either a fine file or emery paper. A base may be fitted to the figure, or holes can be made in a baseboard or flooring, or a stand or support used. When fixing arms in position use a blob of plasticine for support. Plasticine should also be used when fixing the head. A typical figure can be assembled in less than forty-five minutes, although the time obviously depends on the number of parts in the kit and your experience. The steps are the same for any figure and the assembly of the most complex mounted figure is only a matter of time. When the assembly of the figure is completed it should be checked to ensure there is no excess glue left on the surface. This can be filed or sanded off, and the model should then be gently washed with a soft brush in lukewarm water with some detergent added to remove all traces of grease.

On white metal you can use model oil paints which are enamel-based. These are available from model shops in a wide selection of colours. You can also use other paints, either artist oils or watercolours. However, you will need to apply a coat of primer to the metal first. Undercoat in either white or grey is ideal, although emulsion paint can be used. The model must be thoroughly clean before painting, and this can be achieved by washing in detergent. You will also need paint thinners and/or brush cleaner and old cups or cartons for mixing paint. A range of paints is available from model shops, and there are mail order suppliers in the List of Suppliers.

When thoroughly dry the figure is then ready to be undercoated or primed to provide a suitable base for whatever paint finish is to be applied. Undercoat should be thin and even to give a good base without obscuring small detail. Almost any type of paint can be used, depending on the user's skill or inclination. Oil paints are widely used. As a general rule, matt finishes look better than gloss. Watercolours can also be used. If figures are likely to be handled after completion, they should be given an overall coat of matt varnish, when all the colours are thoroughly dry. A number of manufacturers recommend proprietary polyurethane varnish which can be obtained at home decorating shops. It is important to allow the varnish to dry properly.

Phoenix Model Developments Ltd carry one of the best ranges of general and historical figures. As well as military figures there are also large ranges for the English Regency, Georgian and Victorian periods, and the Viking raids and the Second World War. Appropriate furniture ranging from a bible box to a Regency period sofa is also available, as are a variety of accessories. These items have been used in the scenes on pages 115 and 118.

A variation on the white-metal figures are figures made from resin for home assembly. These are superbly detailed and are made up in much the same way as metal figures. They are not, however, suitable for beginners because resin is extremely hard and requires either much manual work or power tools before the pieces can be adequately fitted together, to do justice to the modelling of the kit.

## PORCELAIN AND CHINA DOLLS

The history of dolls' house dolls is a specialized subject in itself. A trip to the Bethnal Green Museum of Childhood reveals that dolls' house dolls can be made from a whole variety of materials such as papier mâché, glazed china, unglazed porcelain, various highly unpleasant-smelling composition formulae and, of course, wood and wax. For the amateur home modeller who wishes to make a satisfactory dolls' house family in small scale, perhaps the best answer is to buy a porcelain kit from one of the suppliers listed at the back of this book.

Modern dolls' houses are usually consistent in their scale. Conversely, it may be difficult to achieve realistic scenes in an old dolls' house because of the variations of scale, and modern figures put into an old house always represent something of a compromise. Whatever scale is used, one should aim for satisfactory proportions once the doll is completely clothed and has hair. In half scale, as a general guide, a man will be

3in (7.5cm), a lady about 2½in (6.5cm) and a child between 1½–2in (3.75–5cm) tall. Like people, not all dolls need be beautiful. A mixture of age groups and weights adds life to a scene. *See*, for example, the beach scenes on page 145. It makes sense to space family ages realistically. It is, of course, always possible to break the rules of scale if one wishes to create a fantasy scene.

Arms can be a problem. As a general rule, the distance from fingertip to fingertip should equal your figure's height. Particularly for male characters, you may need to allow a little extra for shoulders and elbows. If your figure is to be holding a doll or a baby, the arm that crosses the body may need to be made a little longer so that your porcelain baby looks as though it is being held naturally. If a figure is to be sitting or kneeling, you may need to allow a little extra length. This is particularly true in garden scenes.

It is quite possible to make your own porcelain dolls, but the initial outlay on equipment is considerable. This is not recommended without the benefit of professional tuition in the use of kilns, moulds, slip (liquid clay) and paint. Those firms who supply doll-making materials usually also run extremely good courses.

*Choosing a Kit*

One of the best ways of seeing what figures are available in porcelain kits is to attend several of the bigger dolls' house fairs and also to send for mail order catalogues. Price, however, does not necessarily reflect good workmanship. You should consider the following:

- There should be a wide range of realistic heads with clearly defined features, including male figures and children. These should be properly scaled and the finished heads should be free from unplanned defects such as pitting or mould lines. The plaster of Paris moulds

used to make most porcelain dolls wear out over time, and not all dealers are scrupulous about discarding worn moulds.

- The bisque should be appropriately coloured for the type of doll you require and should have a smooth, even finish without any black dots. These are a sign of poor quality slip, or under-firing.

- It is particularly important for half scale and smaller scale dolls that their features, especially their eyes, should be delicately painted and that their mouths and cheeks are not too red. Many a small masterpiece is spoiled by badly painted eyes.

- Arms and legs must be in proportion to the rest of the figure and the hands and feet should be properly defined.

- Small scale figures need to have delicate, slim necks and waist. Ladies who are to wear ball gowns will need suitable shoulder plates and arms.

- If the kit has not been assembled for you, there should be proper means for linking arms and legs to the rest of the figure. The kit should have clear making-up instructions. If in doubt, ask to see these before purchase.

Some figures, particularly male dolls, are sold with moulded hair. You can add hair over this moulding. Most makers sell a variety of feet, including bent or articulated legs, bare feet, boots and even ballet shoes.

Some doll makers will undertake commission work making portrait dolls, but it is worth considering whether there is already a suitable figure in the range. Many old-lady dolls will adapt as a suitable witch, and fairies can be made from small children.

Particularly for small size (half scale and down) dolls, doll makers do offer a making-up service so that the body comes ready to dress. Porcelain dolls are fragile and it makes sense to work so that they are not shattered by careless handling. Mistakes can be removed by soaking.

## MAKING UP BODIES

### Making up Dolls' House Dolls

Many of the suppliers of dolls' house doll parts sell old-style reproductions of traditional Victorian dolls, including those that came ready fitted with their own hats and bonnets. Genuine antique dolls' house dolls are collected and are valuable. You should not alter or clean these without professional advice. Reproduction of Victorian-style dolls' bodies are usually made from cotton or calico, or even felt. The method is simple:

1.  Cut out two squares with sides wide enough to go around the top of the arms and provide a seam allowance, and two to fit the legs. Slight shaping will be needed to allow room to turn the right side out.
2.  Fold the fabric in half and sew or stick down the long side, shaping at one end so that it will fit closely over the top of the limb.
3.  Insert the limb at the wide end, so that the seams will be at the underarm or at the centre at the back of the leg.
4.  Secure by winding strong thread, such as button thread, several times around the limb just below the ridge, finishing with a tight knot and some glue.
5.  Gently pull the tube back over the limb and stuff with a little dry sawdust.
6.  Stitch across to make elbow or leg joints, and then add more sawdust to the upper legs but leave the upper arms almost empty.
7.  Cut two squares for the body. Tack the arms on to the top of each side of the square, and the legs on to the bottom edge.
8.  With the right sides together, stitch the front to the back body leaving the bottom edges open.
9.  Turn the right side out, stuff firmly with sawdust and stitch the bottom edge closed.

10. Glue the shoulder head to the body.

I need hardly point out that these dolls do not stand satisfactorily, which is why so many antique dolls spend their lives gazing at the sky, ill in bed or standing to attention on a dolls' stand. It is a choice between authenticity and realism.

### Making up Modern Doll Kits

Modern day porcelain doll kits are made from flesh-coloured bisque. This is once-fired, unglazed porcelain of the sort used for table or ornamental wear. It is very hard and cannot be easily filed. It will, unfortunately, shatter if dropped, though broken fingers and feet can be satisfactorily mended with superglue. Good doll parts should be hollow, and the doll will have either a swivel head, which fits on to the shoulder plate, or a shoulder head in one piece. Arms finish somewhere between the wrist and the shoulder, and legs somewhere between the hip and the knee. Sometimes a body is provided and in this case the doll is referred to as being an all-bisque doll. These can be assembled by using elastic or wire, according to the directions.

Some dolls are sold with articulated ball-and-socket joints at the shoulder, elbow, waist, hip, knee and ankle; these are expensive. There are also dolls sold with moulded clothing such as corsets. One of the advantages of using a modern-style porcelain doll is that the doll can be made up so that it can be posed in a natural fashion. The figure should be able to stand, hold bits and pieces such as baskets, and kneel or sit. Particularly with half scale dolls, it is important that the waist should be fine to begin with. Added padding can always be put on later.

A simple way of making a body for a doll which does not come with an all-bisque body is to use pipe cleaners. You will need three packs of cleaners, about a metre of polyester wadding cut into a ¼in (6mm) strip, some tacky glue, wire cutters or power scissors, and a ruler. Particularly if this is the first kit which you have made up, start by drawing a pin-man picture to show the proportions of your figure. The method is as follows:

1. For adults, glue a pipe cleaner into each leg and each arm. The length from sole to sole should be 5¼in (12cm) for a man and 4¼in (10cm) for a woman.
2. The height in half scale should be about 3in (8cm) for men, about 2⅜in (7cm) for women and 2in (5cm) for children.
3. Leave to one side until the glue is set.
4. Hold the middle of the two pairs of limbs and, if you are using shoulder plate and shoulder head, bind them with a pipe cleaner.
5. Check that the limbs are matched properly and that the shoulder plate is in contact with the shoulders.
6. Bind the body from the hips upwards with a strip of wadding, working in a figure of eight around the neck, until there is sufficient thickness to support the shoulder plate.
7. Apply glue liberally to the inside of the shoulder plate and to the pipe cleaners which fit into the head.
8. Seat the head on the body, tipping it slightly forward so the eyes will not be staring straight upward.

A swivel head will have to be attached to the shoulder plate first with strong, thin elastic as follows:

1. Starting from under the shoulder plate, thread the elastic up through the central hole. If the head has two holes at the top, go up through one and down through the other and back through the neck and shoulder plate. If it is open at the top, secure the elastic by threading it through a small bead, or knotting it round a piece of pipe cleaner.

2. Tie the ends of the elastic tightly round the fold point of the prepared limbs. The head will then be attached firmly and able to swivel.
3. Bind the body with wadding strip, starting from just below the waist, winding round and under the shoulder plate until it is the right shape.
4. Bind and stitch the wadding to hold it in shape, adding extra pieces to build the required shape.
5. To add additional strength once the model is complete, paint the wadding with dilute tacky glue.

For the small scale modeller, there are a number of other alternatives to modelled porcelain or metal figures. Moulded plastic parts are sold by suppliers of half scale dolls' house materials and by garden railway suppliers. These figures are either ready to dress, ready dressed or available as an assortment of rather gruesome body parts which can then be joined together with suitable glue. Whenever purchasing these figures, check with the supplier as to the kind of glue or cement which should be used for assembly. These figures may be dressed either in conventional fabric or in paper. Alternatively, clothing can be modelled directly on to the body by the use of epoxy putty such as Milliput.

## HAIR AND CLOTHES BRING CHARACTER TO DOLLS

Traditionally, dolls' house dolls have been dressed in scaled-down versions of real human clothes. It is not hard to see how dressing dolls' house dolls, particularly in Victorian times, was used as a way of instilling needlework skills into otherwise reluctant little girls. This may also account for the superiority in numbers of female dolls over male dolls. Not only were the juvenile seamstresses training to make their own clothes, but men's clothes and uniforms were traditionally made outside the domestic setting by professional tailors. There are, however, other ways to dress figures for miniature scenes. Essentially, clothing can either be made separately from fabric or paper and applied to a premade figure, or the clothing can be made as an integral part of the figure. I describe both methods below.

*Clothing from Fabric and Paper*
The dolls' house world is liberally supplied with artists who dress dolls in the most common collector's scale of ½ scale. There are excellent books of patterns and individual patterns supplied by those tradesmen and craftspersons who also supply special material and minuscule trimmings and buttons for miniature dressmaking. The books that I have found particularly helpful are listed in the Bibliography. Patterns from these books can be reduced on the photocopier or by the squaring-down process . In translating patterns from ½ scale to half scale, it should be borne in mind that it may be necessary to adjust the fabric to be used. The equipment for fabric and paper dressmaking can be obtained from department stores, stationers or by mail order. Sewing needles need to be clean and sharp.

While machine stitching is suitable for hems, particularly where the stitching is to be covered by stuck-on trimming, it can still be overwhelming on seams and careful attention must therefore be paid to matching thread to fabric, or to the use of a tacky glue. Very fine threads should be used, such as 180 polyester. Invisible thread has some afficionados, although personally I have found it to be rather springy. Very sharp scissors should be used, which should be kept only for cutting for miniature work. Do not use paper-cutting scissors and fabric-cutting scissors interchangeably. A few sharp pins (brass lace-making ones are good), tweezers or forceps and a glue bottle or syringe are essential. To mark fabric or paper use either pencil or a quilter's pen which will fade in sunlight.

Some sort of storage system for small bits and pieces is essential. Use free packaging from the supermarket, plastic bags or a purpose-made storage system such as the craft boxes available from Lakeland Limited. A product known as 'Fraycheck', which can be painted on to fabric, is invaluable, as is iron-on lightweight interfacing. Tacky glue, either Aileens or De Luxe, is recommended for this work. The best way to use it on fabric is to paint a very thin line using a glue bottle on each piece. Wait until the glue is tacky and then press the two items together. Glue can also be used to fix trimmings, bows and silk roses.

No glue bottle or syringe has yet been designed which does not occasionally become blocked. It is better to leave the bottle or syringe partly full, possibly with the cap on the end, if this is supplied. If it has been unused for some time, it will still block up but hot water and a needle will usually resolve this problem. You will also need a small pressing board: a sleeve board and a steam iron is ideal. I also use a pressing mitten.

*Fabrics*
The finest of silks and cottons can be difficult to handle in half scale or below. Avoid any fabric which frays or is loosely woven. Fabrics with a starch-like finish may be softened by washing and it is sometimes possible to use parts of an old item from a jumble sale or charity shop. Gathering is not a possibility in small scales, and draping or pleating often requires the use of a fabric stiffener. Sari silk is particularly useful, when carefully treated to prevent fraying, as it is so fine. Another way to achieve a reliably draped or pleated look is to use a very fine interlining or tinfoil. Both of these can also be used to provide extra stiffness for hat brims and bonnets.

*Interior, Sherlock Holmes room box.*

### Trimmings

Trimmings are an essential part of both miniature dressmaking and miniature furnishing. Narrow Picot braid is particularly useful, as are the braids sold for egg decoration. Lampshade braid can provide narrow corded trimming, if you unpick it. The only ribbon which is really satisfactory in small scales is the pure silk sort sold for ribbon embroidery.

Another very useful product is Bunka braid sold by egg-craft suppliers. This is, I believe, used to make lampshade braid commercially, but its uses in miniatures are manifold. If unpicked it can be used according to colour for hair and flowers, and as a trim in its own right.

There are many fine pleated ribbon and lace trimmings which can be used to make clothing in their own right.

A word of warning: most white lace made from artificial fibres looks too new and bright in a period setting. Use diluted cold tea or coffee to give it a more attractive colour. Lace can also be painted or dyed, if

it is made from cotton or rayon. Nylon lace does not take colour well. Use only really tiny beads or gemstones. The best selection is carried by suppliers of materials for egg crafters. In particular, Tee Pee Crafts have very tiny gemstones and beads. I have also used small pieces of broken jewellery and pieces of brass fretwork from model railway building kits. It is sometimes possible to obtain a suitably shaped charm for a fan or handbag. Attractively dyed coloured feathers can be obtained from the suppliers listed in the List of Suppliers.

### Moulded or Integral Clothing

One of the best ways of learning about costume and how to make moulded or integral costume is to assemble a few of the excellent white-metal historical kits supplied by companies such as Phoenix. As described above, these come in a variety of scales but I would recommend starting with the ½ scale range which is available in Regency, Georgian and Victorian style, including a special Sherlock Holmes scene.

# 5

# Furnishings

Good dolls' house or miniature furniture is an art form in itself. Even the large London auction houses must now accept that the supply of full-scale antique furnishing is not endless. In miniature, it is possible for the collector to have complete perfect sets of furniture from any period that he desires. Unfortunately, the best of these will cost almost as much as a full-sized version.

Do not let the wonderful work of John Davenport or Le Chateau put you off making your own furniture. Practice will lead to vast improvements. There are many kits available in all sorts of materials, and a great many craftsmen working in this field in every period and in every material from resin to crochet cotton and pins.

Whether you make or buy your miniature furnishing, anything from a medieval castle to a space-age kitchen can be achieved. From the many fairs which I have attended, it seems that cluttered Victorian, closely followed by Art Nouveau are the most popular styles. It is even possible to create furnishings from items which other people who are not miniaturists throw away. A visit to a museum collection is helpful. Some furniture will be faithful copies of antiques and some will only give the genuine article what one writer has called 'a passing glance'.

In the last fifteen years, collecting miniature furniture, particularly in $\frac{1}{2}$ scale, has become enormously popular. Commercially available furniture starts with ranges of beautiful museum quality pieces, such as those made by the Turners and by John Hodgson. Also generally available are reasonably priced but sometimes rather oddly scaled pieces from Taiwan and Korea.

If you have bought this book, it is likely that you will want to make your own furniture, or at least to improve upon kit or mass-produced items. The basic requirements of dolls' house furnishings are as follows, whatever material you use.

## TOOLS

Working in small scale means using small tools. Most households will already have the items listed below, but if you need to purchase any of them, there are tool suppliers in the List of Suppliers who also attend most miniature fairs. You will need:

- Fretsaw and blades
- Small tenon saw
- Ruler and set square
- Small hammer
- Craft knife with replaceable blades which are sharp enough for the work to be undertaken
- Sandpaper or wet and dry paper
- Appropriate glue
- Scissors, including power scissors
- Tweezers and wire cutters
- Paper for making patterns
- Material to make your furniture from

The material you use does not need to be wood. Both laminated card and polymer clay can be used to make excellent furniture, and these are often easier for beginners who may be unused to woodworking. Modern kitchen furniture is best made from plastic sheet.

*Interior, dining room cabinet house.*

# WOOD

The timber which you use should be small grained and well seasoned so that it doesn't warp. Though balsa wood is very soft to cut, it is in fact classified as a hardwood. Unfortunately, although it is easy to cut, its grain is rather obvious and this makes it unsuitable for many miniatures. Orange wood is used to make tongue depressors and lolly sticks. Both of these are fine grained and sawn into fine planks. Pre-sawn circles and other wooden shapes can be found in large craft supermarkets. Many miniaturists use pieces of old furniture. For the beginner, a convenient alternative to this is the pre-sawn hardwood sold for miniaturists by firms such as Gran's Attic, Trent Workshop and Wood Supplies. For the novice it is worth noting that some of these woods are so fine grained that they can be cut with a pair of strong scissors. Some books on miniature furniture recommend the use of old cigar boxes. My experience is that these are now made predominantly from card and the paper labels are collectors' items in themselves. Balsa wood can be used as a base to attach veneer. Veneer alone can be used to make furniture for very small scale dwellings.

There are a number of suppliers of machine-cut mouldings, such as skirting board, cornice and shelving. In addition, most general model suppliers and model shops sell a range of Obechi which can be cut with scissors. The same shops also sell a range of doweling which can be used for rails and posts.

Most modellers will find miniature clamps useful, whether they are making their own work or assembling a kit. Also extremely useful are the elastic bands sold for holding children's hair and the clips used by hairdressers.

You will need to use a variety of fine grain sandpapers, all with sand with the grain.

Sanding dust can be conveniently removed with cotton cloth or, better still, with a tack cloth. Items for wood furnishing can be purchased as a kit for beginners from Trent Workshop or, alternatively, from furniture-making suppliers and DIY superstores.

## SECURING TIMBER

As a general rule, few nails are used. Miniature kit suppliers carry a small range of hardware such as drawer pulls and handles, as do dolls' house suppliers. A mail order supplier with a large range is JoJay Crafts.

A guide to the glues commonly used for miniatures is set out on page 20. Always use a syringe or glue bottle to avoid over-use of glue. Remember that the majority of glues are waterproof and projects should therefore be stained before assembly, otherwise you will have large, unsightly, lighter patches on your work.

# CONSTRUCTING FURNITURE

You should, unless you are working from a kit, start with at least a rough plan and preferably one drawn on paper to the exact size. Then proceed as follows:

1. Sand the wood as smooth as possible.
2. Transfer the paper patterns to the wood by tracing and marking out, keeping in mind the way in which the grain lies. You may wish to mark those pieces which are to be cut out as waste.
3. Cut the wood; many miniaturists use a small electric fretsaw.
4. Once all the pieces are cut, they will need to be sandpapered and tried for size to see if they can be properly fitted together.
5. Once everything fits and all surfaces are smooth, the pieces can then be glued together and polished or painted.

To reduce or enlarge a pattern it is possible to use a photocopier, or to square off and reduce the pattern by tracing pattern pieces. Trace the pattern pieces one at a time on to paper and draw a rectangle round each one enclosing the pattern. Divide this rectangle into smaller rectangles and mark them in numerical order and in alphabetical order so that the key points of the pattern can be plotted. Next to this rectangle, draw another grid of the scale to which you wish to reduce your piece and copy this drawing onto this grid.

## PAINTING FURNITURE

Painting dolls' house furniture is crucial; it is the only way in which the majority of DIY-ers can achieve expensive finishes such as marble or lacquer. The various sorts of paints are described, because of their general usefulness, at page 50.

# COLD PORCELAIN FURNITURE

This section is intended to start you making your own $\frac{1}{24}$ scale furniture with very basic equipment. I will start with a word of warning: the Cel Block which I use as a base should not be used for Fimo or polymer clay as it is only suitable for air-drying clay.

Some of the equipment needed is not specific to cold porcelain modelling. A rolling pin and a board to roll the paste out on are required. You will need scissors, paint brushes, colouring, tacky glue, cold cream or Nivea. Cel Craft supply a number of moulds and specialized tools as well as Cel Block. These tools can be used, of course, for other projects. The one tool which I find really useful for all sorts of modelling is the Cel Cake size guide which has a scale ruler in metric and imperial measurements. You will also find ball and needle tools useful.

## BALL AND NEEDLE TOOLS

The metal As i es ball tools are excellent for balling and cupping the paste – ball tools are not suitable for rolling. They are available in a miniature set of six tools (ideal for tiny flowers and the like), several medium sizes (most frequently used) and a large size, suitable for large roses and orchids, and so on. The ball tools are used to thin and soften petal and leaf edges and, the larger the size, the smoother the softening will be. To cup petals and leaves, place on a Cel Pad and roll from the outside of the petal toward the centre. The 'wire' needle tool can be used to both frill and vein petals. Note that it has a squared end and a rounded end. To vein a petal, place the paste on a rolling board or Cel Pad, and roll over the surface, back and front, with the squared end of the needle tool. Work from the middle outwards so as not to distort the shape; veins normally radiate out from the centre at the base of the petal. The finest needle tool will give the finest veins, so for heavier veins use a thicker needle tool. To frill, rest the petal on an index finger or the edge of a Cel Pad and hold the needle tool at an angle so that the point will not dig into the surface of the petal. Work back and forth, frilling the petal edge as required, always working from the centre outwards to retain the petal shape. Frilling is vital to give movement to fabric and plants, and so is worth practising.

To pattern and texture the paste, I have also used embossing tools available from Holly Products and for the Victorian blue suite I have used a set of oval cutters that are available from most cake decorating shops (*see* the Half Scale Hotel on page 139).

## BEDROOM SUITES

The headboard is made from cold porcelain rolled into a sheet and then pressed into Cel Craft's Lattice Extension Mould. You will need to use the smaller of the rectangular pieces, which gives a textured basketwork effect. You can either paint the headboard after the paste has dried or pre-colour your paste by kneading in a small quantity of gouache. Cut a block of Cel

*Interior, half scale hotel bedroom.*

Block measuring 3½ by 2½in and ½in in height (89 × 64 × 13mm). From white or pre-coloured paste cut a strip to fit round the bed as a valance. This should be 12in (305mm) in length and ½in in depth. Frill the strip with a 'wire' needle tool used on a Cel Pad. Arrange the valance round the bed base with a small ball tool. Press it down on to the pre-glued top edge.

The quilt is made by cutting an oblong of paste 3½ by 2½in and about ¼in (6mm) thick from pre-coloured rolled-out paste. A pattern is stamped on this and the edges frilled with a needle tool. The pillows have been made by shaping a Size 10 ball of paste into a rectangle and frilling the edge. If you want an untidy bed, then the pillows and quilt can be appropriately arranged before painting.

A simple nightshirt, nightie and shawl can be made by cutting shapes from finely rolled paste and frilled hems and cuffs. The small cushions are made in the same way as the pillows from smaller painted pieces of paste. The two heart-shaped cushions are made from an Amaco Push Mould. The patterns on the material are achieved by careful painting even if you pre-colour your paste. I used turquoise for the quilt. You can antique your embossed quilting and also dry-brush the finished result. Do not dry-brush until the paste is completely dry. Pearlized colours look like silk or satin. Depending on the base colour used, you can achieve a variety of effects. White with coloured pearlized paint will give just a subtle hint of colour. Use the same pearlized paint over a dark colour and you can achieve really rich iridescent colours which are particularly appropriate for grand room sets and, indeed, Victorian ladies' frocks.

The bedroom chairs are made in the same way as the sitting-room chairs. A dressing table is simply built over a block of Cel Block ¾in high by ¾in by 1½in (19 × 19 × 38mm). Cover this with frilled paste in the same way as the bed and then drape

two oval shapes from finely rolled paste. Using a ball tool, frill out the edges to look like lace. The mirror is a simple oval of paste with a twisted rope edge from a Cel Block mould used as a frame. This makes excellent picture frames as well.

## VICTORIAN-STYLE SUITE

I cut very simple and rough shapes with rounded corners 1¼in by 1in for the sofa and ¾in square for the chairs. The frilled base was added as for the bed. The edge of the suite is made by pre-formed moulding with a Greek key pattern. You could use any of the small moulding strips in Cel Craft's moulds. Frilled ovals cut with a cutter were used to form the back and seat for the sofa. I added another smaller oval with a design stamped in it and made two small oval cushions in the same way as the bed cushions.

## THE MODERN SUITE

This is made from a block of Cel Block 1in by 2in and ¾in high (25 × 51 × 19mm). I have covered three sides of the block in brown pre-coloured paste and then cut an oblong which is formed over a piece of tin foil measuring approximately 5in by 1½in (127 × 38mm) as shown in the diagram. The valance is marked by a needle tool and I put a plastic ½4 scale figure on the sofa while it was still drying to give a saggy sat-on look. Once dry, I polished the sofa with a little beeswax to get a leather effect. The pouffe is a small cube of Cel Block ¾in square and about ½in deep covered with pre-coloured paste and waxed when dry. I 'buttoned' this with the blunt end of a needle tool. You may find this a useful technique for Chesterfield-style sofas. The wicker-look chairs, table and sofa with matching bed are made with Cel Cake's Lattice Extension Mould.

All the finished cold-porcelain furniture can be seen in the hotel rooms on page 140.

# Tips on Using Cold Porcelain

- It is very important that you wash your hands before starting to model to avoid the paste becoming grubby. Because the paste contains glue it quickly picks up dirt and fluff.

- If the paste feels a bit firm before you start to work, it can be warmed up. An unopened pack can be placed in a sink of warm water for a few minutes or paste that is well wrapped can be put on the top of a warm radiator for a little while. Rub a little cold cream on your hands before starting to work the paste. Knead a small amount of paste by hand just before you use it.

- If the paste appears too soft, expose it to the air for a few minutes and knead it, and it will firm as the moisture evaporates. Store the paste in a sealed polythene bag inside a plastic container with a tight fitting top and do not refrigerate or freeze it.

- Large pieces would normally not be made from solid paste because the surface will crack. For a central bulk use styrofoam or papier mâché which may be fixed and supported by strong wires (14g, 18g, etc.). For branches or other thin shapes the wires can be wrapped with absorbent paper (such as toilet paper) before adding the paste. Extra soft paste (paste with water added) may be added to a dried area and blended by rubbing over with wet fingers without leaving noticeable joins.

- To prevent pieces curling whilst drying, turn them over from time to time. It may be necessary to place some flat pieces between two sheets of blotting paper to even out the drying process on both sides.

- I wax my pieces for a leather look with pure beeswax or, for a gold look, with Liberon gilt cream. Sophisticated furniture polish does not seem to work well on cold porcelain.

*Shot of modern chair and pouffe made from cold porcelain.*

49

# 6

# Building Your House

## INTRODUCTION

Whether you plan and build your houses from scratch or buy ready-constructed shells, you will wish to fulfil the basic shell's potential and express your ideas and creativity by decorating your house or building both outside and in. The techniques set out below are not difficult, but do require patience. One of the basic rules of miniature modelling is that, in order to achieve a satisfactory model, one must employ either patient time-consuming work, or money!

Many of the suppliers of dolls' houses and fixtures and fittings for dolls' houses and miniatures sell a wide range of admirable finishing products. These range from brick paper to authentic minuscule real bricks and from modern wallpaper to hand-cast and finished architectural fittings such as pillars and coving. These items are generally excellent for their purpose and of particular use to the beginner. However, they are expensive if you wish to use the best quality products. There is an additional, less obvious difficulty. If you wish to produce the kind of authentic and individual model which will become a family heirloom, then the only way in which you will achieve this is to learn and practise some of the basic techniques set out below. Ready-made products, if used in too great a quantity, do not give the same degree of authenticity and individuality.

The best way to produce dolls' houses that look like real houses, particularly if you are aiming for historical accuracy, is to study and model real buildings. As well as visiting museums and raiding the public library, it is useful to photograph or draw actual buildings. Drawings do not have to be grand, nor do you need to be an expert photographer. A day out with the family to a stately home can be combined with research into the exterior and interior of the house, and you may well find useful guidebooks and postcards on sale. Most stately homes also carry a stock of useful books on local history, furniture, china, costume and even food.

The best paints to use for a beginner are artists' acrylics and watercolours. Opaque paint is useful for internal decoration and external decoration. This can be obtained from art shops, from specialist hobby ceramic suppliers, by mail order and from craft supermarkets and stationers. Another source of small quantities of matt paints is the sample pots sold by DIY supermarkets. These are particularly useful for modern scenes, although some DIY suppliers now also supply ranges of historically accurate colours. For subtle variations in colour, it is better to use watercolours, since they are transparent and can be easily thinned. If you are starting from scratch, the following will be the most useful colours: Chinese white, black, Davy's grey, charcoal grey, raw sienna, raw umber, light red, cadmium red, cadmium yellow, ultramarine and a green such as terre verte or sap green.

Peter Clark sells a range of card for bricks and slates which is particularly useful and reasonably priced for beginners. Also available from mail order suppliers are sheets of plastic or rubber cladding.

# BRICK

Houses can be made in a variety of materials, but one of the commonest is brick. The pattern in which bricks are placed or laid depends on the age or type of wall. Modern cavity wall buildings are constructed in stretcher bond, while older buildings use Flemish or English bonds with bricks laid across the wall (called 'headers') to strengthen them. Traditionally, walls which can be seen from both sides, such as those in walled kitchen gardens, have a special garden wall bond. One of the limitations of commercial brick papers is that they cannot accurately represent the corners of brick-built buildings or the variations of colour. Even if bricks begin their life all the same shade of terracotta, which is frankly unlikely, time will vary colouring. This is in part a product of wear and tear and partly due to natural factors such as moss and lichen. To produce an accurate model, you have a choice between purchasing commercial facing materials (*see* the List of Suppliers) or scribing and painting the bricks yourself. Alternatively, you could cut brick shapes from card. Scratch or emboss the horizontal lines, or course the bricks apart using a modelling blade, then emboss the vertical gaps between the bricks with a small screwdriver.

When you have embossed all the brickwork, you should paint it with a thin coat of mortar-coloured paint over the entire wall. For authenticity, vary the colour. Once the mortar colour has dried thoroughly, paint the bricks individually in a variety of shades. The basis of brick colour is light red or terracotta, with small quantities of umber, sienna or grey added. To age brick, apply a thin coat of transparent brown wash or antiquing wash. Load the brush with paint, brush it into crevices and then wipe it back to highlight the brickwork.

The final stage is to weather the brickwork by dry-brushing shades of green and brown. Dry-brushing is achieved by loading a stiff brush, and then wiping most of the paint off to leave an almost dry brush. Stroke the brush lightly across the surface so that it partially highlights, rather than evenly coats, your work.

# STONE WALLS

Stone is one of the oldest building materials. The stone used varies in shape and surface texture very considerably, and can be represented in a variety of ways. I generally use scribed card for smaller scales and air-hardening clay in grey or white for larger scales (half scale and upwards). The technique to apply Das or other air hardening clay to a building is as follows:

1.  Do not try to cover the whole of a wall at once. Cover an area of about 2in (5cm) square with strong tacky glue; the sort that is described as designers' glue is particularly useful.
2.  Allow the glue to become slightly dry, then apply Das either by pressing it flat with your hands or by rolling it out into a sheet; do not attempt to use a layer thicker than a centimetre (½in), as too thick a layer will lead to cracking.
3.  Gradually cover your model until you have completed a wall.
4.  Scribe the wall with the appropriate pattern.
5.  Carry on in the same way until all the walls have been covered.

N.B. If the Das begins to dry, it can be made workable again by adding a few drops of water.

Do not cover doors or windows. Use a knife or modelling tool to form clean edges around these and other fixtures.

*Exterior, part of Tudor village.*

A wire brush or a toothbrush can be used to texture. The stone pattern will need to be smoothed after embossing and drying with a small scriber, or a file if necessary. You will need to vary the depth of embossing to suit the age and conditions of your wall.

Stone walling is available as embossed plastic and rubber cladding from specialist suppliers and clay stone pieces can also be obtained. Some modellers have used a mixture of polyfiller and glue successfully.

The first stage in painting stone is to apply a thin wash of mortar colour, vary-ing the shade and remembering that old mortar is darker than new. When this is dry each stone can be painted with different shades of the basic stone colour. This will depend on the geology of the original source of the stone. Whether or not you are copying a real building, you will find Matthew Rice's book *Village Buildings of England* an invaluable resource. Remember that in all old buildings local materials are used. Stone colours can be mixed from white, grey, sienna and umber with touches of red and green. Once the main colours have dried, antique as for brickwork and apply weathering by dry-brushing brown, grey and green into the wall. Particularly in towns and industrial areas, buildings will have been darkened by pollution and soot. This can be reproduced by dry-brushing black paint on to raised areas. Lichen can be reproduced by paint and moss by sponge modelling material from model railway suppliers mixed with water-coloured paint, or by using craft dust or pastels in smaller scales.

# HALF-TIMBERED BUILDINGS

There are examples of half-timbered buildings all over England; for authentic Tudor buildings I recommend a visit to Stratford-on-Avon. The basic framework would have been made from two pieces of tree trunk joined together in a cruck frame which is shaped like an inverted 'V'. Additional timbers would be added to form walls. Panels

*Exterior, watermill in Tudor village.*

were then inserted between the walls. The walls used to be made from wattle and daub, although subsequently brick and, in some cases, stone rubble or a mixture of materials known as 'cob' were used.

Brick or stone can be represented as described in the two sections above. Timber is usually represented by wood, particularly balsa wood, and the plaster finishing can be achieved by paint. There are a few modellers who use real plaster for this purpose; one of these is Little Treasures. I represent plaster by painted wood (see page 53). Plaster does not remain white: original plaster was a lime- and water-based mixture which was more grey than white, and was often coloured with iron oxide to make it more attractive. This can be achieved by tinting white acrylic paint with raw umber, burnt umber and a touch of red or grey. Do remember that plaster becomes damp, and attracts mould and damp marks. These can be represented by appropriately coloured paints or, in larger scales, by railway modelling foam or scatter material.

# DOORS, WINDOWS, GUTTERS, DOWN PIPES, ETC.

As well as purchasing doors ready-made, they can be made from card, wood or metal scribed or embossed to represent planks or panels. Door frames can be made from appropriate wooden mouldings. Door knobs can be made from appropriate beads or railway modelling parts, or bought ready-made. Even panel pins can be pressed into service. Hinges, handles and latches can be made from bent wire or cut metal or bought ready-made. External hinges can be purchased or cut from thin sheet metal. I have often used wine bottle tops cut with tinsnips or strong scissors.

Windows are usually made from thin transparent plastic sheet. In larger scales – half scale and upwards – stained glass can be achieved by painting on the plastic with glass colours. Lead effect can be achieved by indelible ink, photocopying patterns directly on to overhead projection film, or with liquid lead which is in fact thickened acrylic paint coloured to look like lead. This can be applied directly from the tube, rather in the manner of icing a cake. For quarter scale and below, commercially printed stained glass is available from Langley Models. Window frames can be made from card or wood, or purchased ready-made. Commercially available gutters and ironwork can be bought, or made from thin brass sheet pressed into a groove. Down pipes can be made from wire or plastic extrusion.

# ROOFING MATERIALS

### THATCH

Real thatch is made from wheat straw or reed. Wheat straw is relatively coarse and the length of the fibres can be seen. Reed presents a finer, denser appearance and only the end of the fibres show. A variety of materials have been used by modellers to simulate thatch, including coir, plumbers' hemp, pieces of mops and brushes, bathroom loofahs and rubberized horsehair. Thatch can also be simulated with Das or other modelling mediums. The roof is painted with thin washes of acrylic colours, depending on the age of the roof; a new roof would be a rich golden yellow, but quickly weathering to a dull light brown, and an old roof would be dark brown with possible areas of lighter thatch where it has been repaired. Thatch attracts all sorts of insect life and vegetable growth in the way of mosses and lichens. For authenticity, once your basic colours have dried, add

*Thatched cottage.*

greens and browns, and antique the finished result.

## TILES AND SLATES

Tiles and slates can be bought ready-made in miniature, which is an expensive but very satisfactory solution; ready painted by the sheet as tile paper, cheap but always recognizable; or made by yourself from card. I find the grey board at the back of writing pads and loose-leaf-file paper satisfactory. Cut short strips of tiles and glue them on to the roof in overlapping rows for slates. Some should be glued out of line and/or chipped by cutting off the corners. Satisfactory slates can also be made from price tickets. Tiles and slates should be painted with an overall wash in the appropriate colour, and then picked out as for brickwork and antiqued. Moss and lichen can be added if you wish.

The finishing touch for your roofs is a chimney stack with a chimney pot, and sometimes fancy gingerbread work. If a chimney stack is not to be bricked, I often paint mine with textured acrylic, with carefully washed and sieved sand added. Chimney pots can be made from dowel bought ready-turned from wood, or even made in clay or Das, or they can be brought from suppliers of dolls' house ceramics.

# DECORATIVE PLASTERWORK

Decorative plasterwork adds character to models although, before Victorian times, it was generally more appropriate to rather grand houses than to traditional cottages. The suppliers of plasterwork for miniaturists generally supply their products in ½ scale and in plaster. If you wish to undertake your own architectural plasterwork, assuming that you do not have the necessary skills to make your own moulds, there are many moulds intended for decorative sugar work of the sort that appears on wedding cakes that are suitable. These can be used to cast plaster of Paris, though with the disadvantage that the resulting model will be fragile. You may wish to use a relatively new modelling material called 'Cold Porcelain' (*see* page 45). This can be easily worked and used for repeat motifs in a sugar-craft mould. Plasterwork can be used either externally or internally, and coloured and painted in a variety of ways, including watercolour, oil colour, craft dusts and pastels.

As can be seen from the photograph on page 138, a quick and effective way of decorating a less grand house is to cut motifs from embossed wallpaper or paper doilies. These can then be painted with acrylic paints and antiqued with a wash of water or oil colour before fixing them to your model with strong glue.

# 7

# Miniature Gardening and Landscaping

Although I enjoy gardening, I find gardening magazines and gardening books a mixed blessing. I never seem to catch up with the list of jobs they specify as being absolutely essential for the month or, worse still, the week. Some of the pest control articles are quite frightening! Miniature gardens have much to recommend them. They can reflect the history of gardening and of great plant hunters like the Tradescants. I can grow plants which would never bloom together and incorporate features which are impossible in full scale, given the limitations of a London back garden. If you want a knot-garden, a parterre, a belvedere, pavilions, statues or fountains, then miniature gardening is for you. A little gardening or landscaping comes into many miniature projects. Most of my houses have vegetables or fruit to eat, the odd pot plant, a bunch of flowers, creepers of one sort or another up the side, a tree, or even a complete playground for minuscule children. Building mistakes (well, I make them even if you don't!), cracks, places where the paint didn't take or the varnish did, can all be covered up or improved by the addition of a little graceful foliage. Garden items in this book range from a greengrocer's and plant stall to an outdoor party to celebrate an engagement, complete with herbaceous border and bird bath. If you have a taste for the grotesque, then the landscaping instructions for the Hallowe'en house should be useful. Because gardening and water are so closely connected, I have included a beachscape and an underwater scene in a fish tank among the projects.

In addition to the suppliers listed at the back of this book, there are other less obvious sources of useful material. Your local supermarket will yield a variety of useful items. Pan scourers come in a range of rather lurid greens which can be toned down with the use of paint, and then cut easily into hedges and topiary. They are also much improved by the application of glue and railway scatter material (*see* below). Greenhouses, cold frames, Edwardian cases and cloches can all be made from packaging material. It is sensible to keep a 'bits box' into which should go shampoo bottle tops, pizza supports, corks, scrap canvas, old sheeting and toothpaste tops along with all the other items that miniaturists find useful.

Another useful source of supply is shops and mail order suppliers that specialize in items for cake decorating and sugar craft. There is a section below on making cold porcelain vegetables, flowers and trees. This useful modelling paste can be coloured very easily and rolled very thinly. With it will be sold a selection of green and brown wire. Modelling tools including leaf veiners and special tools for texturing not only leaves and petals, but bricks and stonework. Cake-decorating shops also sell florists' tape (for pot plants) and florists' ribbon which is useful for large pot plants such as Swiss cheese plants. Many cake-decorating shops also sell small dried flowers such as maidenhair fern (natural and green). They may also sell small silk flowers and stamens.

Railway modellers take modelling landscapes extremely seriously, and good railway model shops will have a section devoted entirely to landscaping supplies. This will include materials such as cork, brick and stone paper, brick and stone plastic sheet and tiles, all sorts of scatter material, trees in various scales, dried natural materials such as reindeer moss, bushes, various creatures to place in your landscape and a wide range of books. Model shops, especially those that cater for railway modellers, are a useful source of specialist adhesives and plaster bandage for constructing valleys and hills, and smaller humps and bumps. Most model shops also sell casting resin and other ways of simulating water for fountains and pools. For statues, particularly classical ones, stands, bits of fountains, twiddly bits and even small flowers, not to mention a wide range of paints, consult an egg-craft supplier's catalogue such as Tee Pee Crafts.

Lastly, there is a number of specialist dolls' house and miniature suppliers who are dedicated to supplying the necessaries for your miniature garden or other landscapes. Of course, individual items can also be used in other projects such as a seaside scene or a park or even a trip to the zoo.

*Dome garden with cat and pink flowers.*

# GARDEN/LANDSCAPE PROJECTS

You do not have to have a house at all in your miniature project. I list below a number of items which you might wish to make a project around with suggestions as to how these might be achieved. These are in alphabetical order for ease of reference:

## ALCOVE

An alcove is a recess in a wall or gatepost used to hold a statue or a bust, or as a seat; where it is used as a beehive, the alcove is called a beebole. Alcoves made of plaster or resin can be bought commercially, or a simple alcove can be made from polystyrene or modelling clay.

## ALLEY

An alley is a broad path cut through trees, the branches of which may be trimmed. Tree-making instructions of all sorts regularly appear in model railway magazines. The individual trees required for projects are detailed below as appropriate to the project concerned.

## AVENUE

An avenue is a broad road lined on both sides with trees planted at regular intervals. The most popular trees would have been lime and horse chestnut.

## ARBOUR

An arbour, sometimes called a bower, is the smallest and most ancient of garden houses, dating back to at least the middle ages. It is a shady retreat large enough for a seat and often covered by climbing plants. These can be easily constructed from wood, plastic canvas, tapestry canvas, wicker or any other trellis material, and can also be purchased ready-made.

## AVIARY

An aviary can be part of a zoo or a feature in a grand stately home garden. It is also a useful way to use up interestingly-shaped packaging such as plastic trifle dishes (back to the supermarket!). Suitable plastic curlicues can be obtained from cake icing shops or made from cold porcelain. Peter Clark makes lovely exotic birds. These are also to be seen sold by other suppliers at dolls' house fairs.

## ARCADE

An arcade can be a series of covered shops, but it can also be a series of connected arches which may make a focus for an outdoor scene. The best way of making one of these is to use pre-formed railway arches such as those sold by Langley Models and to follow the general instructions for painting stone or brickwork.

## BASIN

A basin is the receptacle which collects the water from a fountain. You will see an example in my Roman garden on page 154.

## BALUSTRADE

A balustrade is a row of banisters or small pillars supporting a coping or a small parapet. There is an example of this in the party

*Dome garden with garden chair and flowers.*

house. It is a common feature of Georgian buildings and you can see an example on page 131.

## BATHHOUSE

I have yet to see a project including a bathhouse, which is anything from a small sunken pool to something exotic such as a spa baths at Bath or Harrogate.

## BELVEDERE

A belvedere is a lookout tower commanding views of the surrounding countryside. These were functional up to the middle ages, but gradually became purely ornamental.

## BOLLARDS

Bollards are short posts made of stone, cement or wood, set at regular intervals to prevent the entry of animals or vehicles into a restricted area. Many stately homes have cattle grids to keep their livestock from straying. I have never seen a cattle grid included in miniature gardens, although some railway modellers include both cattle grids and their companion, the ha-ha, which is a wide ditch designed to keep animals from straying whilst not spoiling the view in the way that a fence would.

## CANAL

A long rectangular water feature in a formal garden is called a canal.

## CASCADE

Some grand stately homes have a cascade with a single substantial jet of water sometimes running down into a waterfall.

## CHINOISERIE

Chinoiserie is the Chinese style popular in Georgian times and subsequently. Famous examples of these can be seen at Stow and at Kew.

## CLAIR-VOYEE

A *clair-voyee* is a wrought-iron screen set into a wall to extend the view. This could be a useful device for the modeller, in that it breaks up a brick wall but allows for a small view, thus giving depth to what otherwise might be a rather flat project.

## CONSERVATORIES

Conservatories have become popular in miniature gardens. These are, like greenhouses, glass-covered structures for tender plants. This is another use for ornate supermarket packaging. There are a number of conservatory kits on sale in a variety of scales. These can be converted into palm houses or, with the additional of pillars,

into orangeries. Orange and lemon trees are supposed to have been the first tender evergreens to be bought back to England, and in winter they were moved into the orangeries of stately homes. They were very much a status symbol, requiring artificial heat to flourish or even survive. Apart from the aspidistra, the other popular Victorian indoor plant was the fern. These used to be cultivated principally in outdoor ferneries which were sometimes combined with a grotto. These are rather fun to make.

## DOVECOTE

One of the oldest garden features is a dovecote. These are brick- or stone-built pigeon houses used to house pigeons or doves. They can be tiny, or quite palatial. To see the grander sort, consult the National Trust Guide.

*Dome garden with statue and yellow lilies.*

## EXEDRA

You may want to use an exedra, which is the technical term for a semicircular expanse of turf, usually with statues on it and with a hedge around forming a curved boundary. This is a convenient backdrop to a romantic scene in the garden. If you wish to create a miniature reproduction of Shakespeare in the park and to use a larger version, an open-air stage of turf with neatly trimmed hedges to form the wings is called a *théâtre de verdure*. This makes an ideal backdrop for one of the scenes from *A Midsummer Night's Dream.*

## FOLLY

By far and away the best escape for the modeller's imagination is the folly. This a general term for decorative but useless structures such as fake castles, fake ruins, half a bridge, pagodas, temples, pyramids, stone circles of the sort favoured by Lord Bath, fake fairy castles, chalets and miniature houses of the sort favoured by wealthy aristocrats. Many of these have been preserved by English Heritage and the National Trust. They make a delightful small project or even a present for a miniaturing friend. There are also useful for a corner project. Garden houses are more practical than follies. They are used to house people rather than plants and the term covers arbours (*see* above) and large structures such as pavilions which aren't only used for cricket. A gazebo is between these two extremes, as is the more recent summerhouse.

## GARDEN GNOMES

Smaller gardens have ornamental wishing wells sometimes with garden gnomes to go with them. Gnomes can be obtained from miniature garden suppliers, or you can use bracelet charms, railway figures repainted and Milliputted, or egg-craft supplies.

## GARDEN SEATS

Garden seats can be made of stone, Fimo, Das, wood, plastic, or even metal. Phoenix sell a kit for a Victorian garden seat.

## GREENHOUSES

A variety of kits exist for making miniature greenhouses, but they are not difficult to make from scratch, particularly from plastic packaging. Both plastic canvas and fretwork can be useful. An example of a miniature greenhouse is shown on page 152.

## KNOT-GARDENS

Knot-gardens have been popular since Tudor times. It is the technical term for a small, diametrically shaped group of beds outlined in clipped hedges, boxes or shrubs with the spaces between filled with flowers or coloured stones. This is an easy project for a first miniature garden. The hedges can be made from pot scourers or oasis with railway scatter material added and the centres filled in with dried flowers. It is technically possible to have a lake or lagoon in a miniature project providing your scale is small enough. You will need to use widely available modeller's water substitutes.

## PAGODA

A pagoda is a particularly fun project.

## PARTERRE

The parterre is a development from the knot-garden. A parterre is sometimes backed by a bosket, which is a block of closely planted trees providing a dark background for the colours of the plants in the parterre. This is also a useful way of avoiding having to draw a detailed background for a miniature garden.

*Drawer garden.*

## PERGOLA

A pergola is an arch structure that supports climbing plants, usually wisteria or rambling roses. Cake decorating pillars are ideal.

## SARCOPHAGUS

This is a stone coffin. Without a lid, it tends to be referred as a cistern. Cisterns are actually intended merely for the collection of rainwater, but the old ones are now used as ornaments or as plant troughs. They are usually made of lead or marble and bear, in the case of the lead ones, a manufacturer's date. Sarcophaguses are made of stone or marble. The lids seem to have survived less well in most cases. Really battered ones seem to get used as horse troughs.

## SUN DIALS

Most minuscule garden suppliers supply sun dials, although these can be easily contrived from small pillars either from cake-decorating shops or egg crafters.

## VASES

There is a huge variety of ready-made vases. These can also be made from Das or Fimo, as can covered vases, which are usually known as urns. Urns tend to be located in grand gardens and be stuck on pillars or walls.

*Another drawer garden.*

## WELL HEADS

Grand gardens have well heads which stand over real wells. These are usually made of stone and cast iron, and are attractive because of their situation rather than their actual appearance.

I began my landscape projects with a corner of a Roman garden prompted by the purchase of a miniature fountain. Gardening, however, did not begin in Rome or in England, despite our long history. The first gardens were in Egypt in the Nile Delta and in China. Gardening spread in the ancient world to Babylon which had hanging gardens, one of the wonders of the ancient world. Through the Middle Ages, English gardens were mainly for growing food and herbs and were associated predominantly with monasteries and castles.

The garden at Hampton Court was started by Henry VIII, who had advanced ideas on gardening as well as marriage and religion. Great English gardening of the sort the country is famous for did not arrive until the eighteenth century. Our garden flowers have developed from cottage garden flowers and the back gardens of industrial workers. It is worth remembering that there were fashions for flowers: the Romans were inordinately fond of roses; fortunes were lost and won later in the golden age of the Netherlands in respect of bulbs, particularly tulips; and no miniature Victorian parlour is complete without its aspidistra, sometimes called the cast iron plant. One of the most enjoyable treats of my childhood was the village fête. This often included a vegetable and flower show. Now there's an idea for a miniature project, but I fear it would take a whole book to describe by itself.

# MINIATURE FLOWERS

Miniature flowers can be made from silk, cotton, plastic, unravelled Bunka braid, dried and paper flowers and from modelling materials such as Fimo and cold porcelain. Using silk, plastic or other flowers from a florist or craft shop is usually a question of disassembly: larger flowers have to be cut down into manageable sections or individual flowerettes. Tiny dried flowers often resemble larger garden flowers. Sundried flowers are dyed, particularly those which are sold at Christmas time in shades of red. Their lifetime can be substantially extended with a coat of spray varnish, which preserves the colour and keeps the dust off. Paper flowers can be bought in kit form or made up from hole punches.

Simple paper flowers can also be made from quilling paper and from rice paper. Rice paper makes beautiful petals because it takes paint, particularly watercolour, unevenly which gives a natural look. The Miniature Garden Centre also sells laser cut leaves suitable as ivy or Virginia creeper. Paint the whole card first – do not attempt to paint individual leaves. Leaves and flowers can also be made using the kind of coloured paper that comes with junk mail and a hole punch. Rubber stamp suppliers sell a variety of punches, although these require a certain amount of lateral thinking. You may, however, find that sun and star punches are small enough.

The basic technique for making silk roses is easily learned. Directions are included with rose makers. The scales of roses can be determined by the breadth and thickness of the ribbon used. Very fine silk ribbon, suitable for small-scale roses, can be obtained commercially.

For finely detailed garden flowers, nothing beats cold porcelain. The techniques shown for use with cold porcelain can be used for Fimo, but it is possible to roll cold porcelain almost to transparency in a way that cannot be achieved with Fimo.

Miniature and micro cutters are available from the suppliers listed at the back of the book. The following are the basics:

- **Blossoms** This is a two-piece set of five and six petal cutters which can used for roses, sweet peas, carnations and pinks.
- **Daffodils** This is a three-piece set for daffodils and narcissus.
- **Daisies** This is a two-piece set usually including flower and leaf, also suitable for chrysanthemums and water lilies.
- **Fuchsias** This is a three-piece set which can be used for fuchsias, lilac, bouvardia and wisteria.
- **Irises** A three-piece set including leaves, which can be used for clovers and shamrock.
- **Orchids** This is a two-piece set.
- **Pansies** A two-piece set which can also be used for violets, violas and so on.

Also available are miniature ivy and fern cutters which can be used for maple leaves and Virginia creeper, and a calix set which, as well as adding authenticity to flowers, can be used to make small blossoms.

As well as cutters you will need a nonstick rolling board, a Cel Pen or other nonstick roller, fine wire, floristry tape, glue and suitable pots. I particularly like Carol Mann's and Clive Brooker's pots. Small-scale terracotta pots are freely available both in terracotta and, from Phoenix, in metal for you to paint. They all look better if their basic terracotta colour is modified with a bit of dirt and moss in the form of antiquing solution and sponged on green and brown paint. Bloom that sometimes affects old flower pots can be imitated by using a very small quantity of liming wax and a cotton bud. Plants can be held in pots by florists' Stay-Soft. Model railway gravel or tea leaves improves the appearance of this.

You will also need floristry tape in different colours, which can be bought from florists and from cake decorating shops, a foam pad such as the Cel Pad, an assortment of gouache and oil paints, craft and/or sugar-craft dusts, and silk and matt spray varnish. As a general rule, vegetables, flowers and any other kind of vegetation should not be sprayed with gloss varnish unless they are naturally shiny, such as camellia leaves. However, if your model is likely to be handled a lot, use gloss varnish. I found that my demonstration flowers and plants stood up well to handling but were covered in fingerprints. Miniature flowers, and indeed full-scale cold porcelain flower making, is now a popular hobby in its own right.

In scales such as quarter scale, O gauge and OO gauge, it is not possible to have very detailed flowers except perhaps for something as large as a sunflower. Modellers use scatter material which is available in a variety of colours, bits of something known as flowering, flexible hedging and dismembered bushes 2cm (1in) high. These are used in conjunction with various sorts of trees, lichen and foliage material. A product called 'scatter grip' made by Deluxe is ideal for applying scatter materials since it remains flexible. A suggestion of different sorts of flowers can be also achieved with coloured sand available from craft and hobby ceramic suppliers, sieved modelling clay used with a clay gun and unravelled braid, such as lampshade trim. In small scales, such as the rows of houses supplied by Cove Models, the gardens and vegetation are often included. All landscapers and potential miniature

gardeners should try to visit the Pendon Museum. Although this is basically a railway layout, the houses and landscaping are exquisite and many products sold in the shop cannot be obtained easily elsewhere. Also available from the Pendon Museum shop are a number of excellent books on miniature landscaping.

All miniature landscaping requires a basic structure and the method for using the plaster bandage and newspaper pad technique, which most model railway enthusiasts use and translates conveniently into most scales, is described on pages 87–8.

# LANDSCAPES

Successful landscape projects depend upon craft skills and observation. A West Country farmhouse is not in the same landscape and surroundings as a Scottish croft. If you visit a model railway show, it is still possible to see landscapes where spring and summer foliage and flowers amazingly seem to bloom together.

First decide upon your buildings, then do your research into the shape of trees, hedges, fences and the walls. Once you have decided on these and decided on your season, particularly if this is your first project, visit a railway shop or obtain catalogues from a mail order supplier. Remember that there are no fixed rules as to what a particular product can be used for. Little bushes may be a fruit orchard in one scale and a pot plant in $\frac{1}{2}$ scale.

The first step with scenery is to build your basic structure. This needs to be strong and self-supporting, and at this stage you must also plan to incorporate features such as roads, railways, water and, of course, the ups and downs of hills and valleys. I use a plaster of Paris-impregnated bandage called 'Modelling Rock' or 'Modrock' and available directly from Hobby's as a basis for scenery. I build on to an under-structure of lumps of expanded polystyrene, balsa wood or crushed newspaper which I use to define my basic shape. Strips of Modrock are laid on to this structure after being dampened with water – it does not need to be soaked. It is absolutely crucial that you do not pour plaster of Paris or Modrock down your sink or drain as they can cause blockages and the attendant large plumbers' bills. The plaster bandage can be modelled whilst it is still wet, if you want to make a ploughed field for your miniature horse. Most paints can be used directly on to the Modrock. I have had some success in using car aerosol paints in greens, greys and browns as a basis for scatter material.

Ready-made instant papier mâché can be useful for landscaping. It has a longer working time than Modrock, up to twenty-four hours, and can be modelled and textured to represent brick, stone or other detailed scenery. Again, it can be painted.

The finishing touch in landscape, particularly in railway modelling, is scatter material. This term covers everything from purchased flock powders or stone chippings to home-made items such as coloured sawdust and dried tea leaves. I use a variety of glues of the whitewood-type and tacky glue. Scattergrip made by Deluxe is very satisfactory too. Brush adhesive on to your model and, before it dries, scatter your scatter material over the wet glued area. Surplus material can be brushed off once the model is dry for further use. Once your basic structure is completed, you will be thinking of weeds, hedgerows and so on. Some of these have already been discussed in the context of gardens. However, for small-scale landscapes, weeds and hedgerow plants are best represented by lichen or rubberized horsehair. There are also a number of plants found in the garden which are worth drying for use as trees or bushes or even flowers.

There are also a number of craft and household items that can be forced into service in landscape. These include oasis foam, florist wire and tape, crumpled polystyrene foam, fur and plush fabric, commercially made silk flowers and dried flowers, string and all sorts of grades of wire. There are a variety of proprietary fencing and walling products, but you can also use any of the following: plastic canvas, tile spacing, craft or lolly sticks, kebab sticks, fruit punnet or orange-box wood, or styrene or plastic mouldings.

Tree bark and cork bark make good model rocks. It is also possible to purchase real sandstone. You may find that chips of deadwood and twigs from real trees, particularly fruit wood are useful. I have already covered the question of wear and tear and antiquing as a means of giving character both to model houses and to furniture; the same techniques are useful for weathering and dirtying landscape. Both antiquing solution and dry-brushing can be used to add dirt, age and grime.

Do remember to take account of the prevailing wind – this is particularly important if preparing a snow scene. Nature is not neat and tidy. Snow scenes are fun to do, particularly for Christmas-village projects. Many dolls' house suppliers now sell grades of artificial snow. However, you could also use a proprietary thickened paint available from hobby ceramic suppliers. Another possibility is to use thickened white paint with glitter sprinkled over it. I appreciate that you may not wish your dolls' house to be a winter or Christmas scene all the year round. Temporary snow can be made by using artificial snow or by using thin layers of quilt wadding mixed with artificial snow and glitter. This can be removed once Christmas is over.

# 8

# Interior Decoration

Few, except the grandest model houses and room boxes, are sold ready decorated. For collectors and modellers, particularly dolls' house people, interior decoration is part of the fun. There is a huge range of products sold for ½₂ scale interior decoration and a rather smaller range of products for half scale modellers. Other crafts, such as parchment craft, stencilling and gilding, can be used to enhance models both in interior decoration and to decorate furniture so that it is part of an integrated scheme. Television programmes such as *Home Front* and *Changing Rooms* as well as the associated magazines have made interior decorating and decorative paint work much less of a mystery. Many of these ideas work just as well in model scales as they do in full scale.

Modern aids such as photocopiers, computers and laser printers can expand the range of wall coverings and fabrics, including carpets, available to the miniaturist.

## USEFUL COMMERCIAL PRODUCTS

The majority of commercially available wallpaper for miniature houses is either modern or Victorian. There are particularly fine selections of William Morris papers. Except for panelling, earlier periods are not well catered for. For floors, printed paper flooring and proprietary cladding and boarding can be obtained. Some craftsmen have a fine range of tiles, though these are expensive. You can save money as well as achieving a greater variety by making your own.

## PAINTING

Decorative painting is not difficult, especially in small scale, and I set out below the basics of colour schemes and techniques.

### COLOUR

Colour is, of course, a matter of personal taste. Light, often assumed to be white, is in fact made up of the seven colours in the spectrum: red, yellow, orange, green, blue, indigo and violet. Objects absorb light: a blue object will appear blue because it absorbs all colours except blue, which it reflects. The laws of physics divide colours into primary colours – red, yellow and blue – and secondary colours – orange, green and violet – which are made by mixing primary colours. The 'colour wheel' has twelve sections: the three primary colours, the three secondary colours and a further six colours which are obtained by mixing primary colours with secondary colours. The colour wheel is useful in planning decorating scenes because you can see the colour at a glance together with its complementary colours (opposites), and whether it is warm and absorbs light or cold and reflects light. Complementary colours appear side-by-side. Primary and secondary colours, if used together, will give rise to distinctly different contrasts.

Harmonious colours can be chosen from those in the colour wheel which are close

*Interior, Half Scale Hotel bedroom.*

together. If you want a contrast, choose diametrically opposite colours. Greater light can be added to a colour by using white; the higher the percentage of white, the more luminous the colour. Intensity is described in terms of shade – as a general rule, use colours of equal intensity to achieve harmony. Mixing base colours in different proportions extends the range of shades available. Most children know that grey can be made by mixing white and black: the shade can be warmed by adding a little ochre or made cooler with the addition of blue. Grey can also be made by mixing two complementary colours in equal parts.

The basic colour mixing rules are as follows:

• To warm a colour, add ochre or umber.
• To cool a colour, add blue.
• To brighten a colour, add white.

- To darken a colour, add black.
- To lighten a colour, for example when adding highlights, add a brushstroke of the same colour with a greater degree of white added.
- To shadow or darken a colour, use the same colour with black or a darker colour added.
- To shade a colour, move gradually from a darker to a lighter colour.

To begin with it is sensible to work out colour schemes on a piece of paper before diving into your project. An easy shortcut is to buy or obtain paint sample cards from a paint shop or a DIY shop. The National Trust sells a range of historically accurate paints, and sample pots of these can be obtained in some National Trust shops and from Farrow and Bell. These products are also sold in some DIY supermarkets.

## PREPARING SURFACES

Both artists and craftsmen know that a good quality paint surface cannot be obtained unless the surface under the paint has been properly prepared. Old paint needs to be removed, wood will need to be sandpapered and may need a coat of primer, and sometimes a decorative paint technique will need a specially prepared base decoration.

## APPLYING PAINT

Paint can be applied with brushes, with sprays, with a sponge, with a rag or even with rolled-up paper. Sponging paint on can be particularly appropriate for miniature projects because brush marks do not show. Use a clean, natural sponge and rotate it to avoid obvious patterns. It produces a soft orange peel effect, which is a useful approximation of old painted plaster work. Natural sponges can be rinsed and re-used. If using a rag or newspaper to apply paint, you will need to bear in mind that these cannot be washed out and therefore a selection of small pieces of rag or balls of newspaper should be prepared.

A finish for paintwork which is particularly useful for posh interiors and kitchens is liming or pickling, which used to be achieved by caustic soda. Today, liming wax will give the same affect – Trent Workshop sell this. Liming wax is particularly attractive over country colours and can be used for walls, floors and furniture. A range of wood stains in a variety of colours is available, which can be either wood- or spirit-based. Small sample pots can be bought.

It is not necessary to paint elaborate pictures on plain painted walls to make them look more attractive or authentic.

Stippling or mottling means applying spots of colour contrasting with a base. This can be achieved by flicking a stencil brush or even an old toothbrush over the surface of the base-coated piece of work. The brush should be held at right angles to the work which should be dry and then the bristles can be flicked with the index finger. Move the arm gradually over the surface to produce uniform mottling. Toothbrushes produce, unless grossly overloaded, the finest, most uniform dots.

I achieve a marble-like finish with a mixture of sponging and veining. Mock marble finishes are the subject of chapters and even whole books on decorative painting.

Decorated surfaces can be finished in a variety of ways. Matt or gloss polyurethane lacquer, applied according to the bottle or can, is the cheapest and most effective. Wax can also be used. Many paint surfaces, particularly those in buildings which are supposed to be old and much used, improve with distressing and antiquing. This is a technique which I have used in the houses illustrated on pages 156–63. I use an antiquing patina which can be diluted with antiquing solution. Antiquing products are available in either water- or spirit-soluble; spirit-soluble versions are obtainable from hobby ceramic suppliers and generally come in a greater range of colours. As oil and water do not mix, a spirit patina can be applied at an early stage in a work composed of multiple colours and then painted over with water-based paints. Water-based patinas should be applied last, otherwise they will be dissolved by subsequent use of watercolour. I always stress when teaching painting classes the need to test out painted finishes on a spare piece of wood or paper before using them on your project.

Wood flooring and panelling should be stained before it is stuck, otherwise the glue will leave an unstainable and unattractive patch. Architectural mouldings can be bought including coving, shelving, picture rail, dados and panelling, to name but a few. Small-scale carving takes real skill and is beyond the scope of this book. A reasonable imitation can be achieved by using cake icing moulds such as those made by Cel Craft or Hawthorn Hill. I use cold porcelain for these purposes as it does not have to be fired in the same way as Fimo or other polymer clay.

Another way of simulating carved ceilings and walls and the occasional panel of furniture is to use embossed paper either bought (examples are embossed dado strip and trims sold for découpage) or made for the purpose by using parchment craft. When using parchment craft for decoration of this sort, it is sensible to use heavier quality parchment. Remember, the parchment can be painted or tinted on its reverse with wax crayons.

There are a number of complex ways of simulating finishes such as tortoiseshell, Chinese lacquer and country French furniture. For the beginner I recommend kits made by Plaid which can be obtained from most hobby supermarkets. For miniaturists this is the only realistic way of buying the necessary colours in small quantities.

# STENCILLING

Stencilling is a very ancient decorative art – it has been in use since 3,000BC in China – which is equally at home on paper, textiles, wood and walls. Stencils may be hand-made from card, metal or overhead projection sheet already purchased. Colour can be dabbed or sprayed or even sponged.

It is appropriate to use simple stencil decorations in Tudor houses and in colonial American room settings. Different patterns were popular in different periods. In the Netherlands, designs were based on leaves, flowers and hearts and, of course, particularly the expensive and sought-after tulip. The Americans quickly borrowed motifs from native American culture. The use of stencils can be seen in books on Art Nouveau and Art Deco. Today, hardly an interiors book or television programme goes out without a section on stencilling.

It is, of course, possible to create co-ordinating wall coverings and fabric by using stencils. Acrylic paint sold by hobby ceramic suppliers can usually be used satisfactorily on wood and fabric, although if you wish to use them on a shiny surface such as glass as well, it would be necessary to add a glass painting medium if the colours are to match.

# RUSTIC AND FOLK PAINTING

American country and German peasant folk-painting and découpage use simple decorations composed of fast and relatively easy paint strokes, and the use of relatively unrefined materials. It can be simulated in miniature quite easily using acrylic paints, sponges and brushes. You will also need antiquing patina and glasspaper to age the decoration, and water-based lacquer or wax to protect it. Country colours tend to be dark: they are intended to be practical and not to show the dirt. Also, before chemical fixatives were invented, these colours lasted longer without fading in sunlight. A country painted room appears on page 110.

Another way of achieving country patterns is to use a country rubber stamp. You may also wish to reproduce the pattern on a simple rug or carpet made from needlepoint canvas, or from cross-stitch material.

# DÉCOUPAGE

Découpage was last in vogue in Victorian times when it was mainly used for scrap screens of the sort shown in the cabinet house on page 119. This is, however, a craft which is enjoying a considerable revival, even to decorate full-sized furniture. Découpage is simple, and a godsend for those miniaturists who are nervous of painting.

# LACQUER

The fashion for Chinoiserie arrived from a taste for lacquered objects usually in black, dark green or Chinese red. These were decorated with colours or shades of gold Chinese-style pictures, and French artists were the first to produce books with images to be cut out, glued and treated with gum lacquer. Chinese-style lacquer work can be easily produced, although not to the same high standard of course, by the use of cellulose car spray.

First, sand down or strip the piece of furniture. Then undercoat with grey or red rust-coloured car undercoat. Finely spray with car paint in black, dark green or Chinese red – Halfords have a wonderful selection of colours. Your design can be either drawn in gold paint or a tiny transfer, or cut from a magazine illustration. As a dedicated miniaturist you owe it to yourself to cut out suitable designs from magazines and newspapers – I find antiques magazines are particularly useful in this respect.

# WALL PAINTINGS, *TROMPE L'OEIL* AND FRESCO

Wall paintings make a miniature room look more opulent and can add depth to a room box. The main reason why these are not used more in miniature projects is, I think, due to lack of confidence rather than lack of talent. Wrapping paper, magazines, holiday brochures, postcards and stately home catalogues can all yield suitable cut-outs which can either be photocopied to enlarge or reduce them, or used 'as is' with a découpage medium such as Modge Podge.

Frescos can be traced or copied from art books. Very simple pictures can add depth to an open door. It is not difficult to paint sea with sky above it. If you do not have room for a bathroom in your dolls' house, then one can be painted.

Wall paintings of the sort popular in Georgian times are often to be found in catalogues from fine art auctioneers. The same catalogues often yield old masters in just the right size, and also a fine selection of half scale carpets, of which more later. It also makes sense to save small cuttings to place on paper plates for displays in a china room wall (*see* page 110).

# GILDING AND SILVERING

Since ancient times mankind has been fascinated by gold. Gold and gilt objects have been found that are as much as three-thousand years old. Those of you lucky to

*Hat shop box showing use of gold and pearlized finishes.*

have been able to see Egyptian antiquities in museums, particularly those dating to Tutankhumen, will know what I mean. Lower cost and the technology to produce gold leaf in ever thinner sheets led to the spread of gilt work to decorate noble palaces and ecclesiastical architecture. In full scale the technique is used mainly to enhance picture frames or special plaster decoration. Gilding is wonderfully effective in miniature for furniture, ceilings, panelling and picture frames, and to add depth and lustre to modelled clothing. There are a variety of gold paints available; for even quicker results, you can use gold waxes which are available in a substantial range of colours, or lustre paste.

It is also possible to obtain books of different coloured metals and gold size from craft supermarkets. Always follow the directions: they do vary from manufacturer to manufacturer. At a first glance, gold wax or gilding would be the more useful, but there are some effects in miniature which can only be achieved by the use of gilding, although one may be using a silverized product. The most obvious of these are the creation of any sort of armour, be it chain mail or plate, antique silver work, door furniture and gilded plaster ceiling. The use of gold can give a sense of opulence to a scene, but can also present a room box in greater depth. A unique anniversary present for either a silver or a gold anniversary is to create a room box or, better still, a house furnished entirely in gold, that is yellows, whites, creams and, of course, real gold or silver, grey, white and pearlized colours.

Toning with gold and silver are pearlized colours. Whilst these are particularly useful for costumes, they are also useful for miniature stately home effects when used over white paint. Pearlized colours, pearl powders and the entire range of glitters also have their uses in fantasy scenes.

71

*Interior, Georgian mansion.*

# 9

# Dolls' House Accessories

A large, well-stocked dolls' house fair is a paradise for enthusiasts, for here they will find the thousands of tiny accessories that convert a furnished dolls' house and its people into scenes full of character and life. I have to admit that ever since my father read Beatrix Potter's tale of *Two Bad Mice* to me and I discovered the delights of plaster dolls' house food, I have made, collected and talked about – sometimes in print – what enthusiasts call 'accessories'. Even if you do not want a dolls' house, and find model trains and aeroplanes immensely boring, it is just possible that a collection of miniature silver or Cranberry glass will give you enormous pleasure. I collect, or perhaps I should say the miniature occupants of my houses collect, teapots, English and French china, miniature books, Cranberry and blue glass (I don't even want this in full scale – I always have clumsy cats and clumsy children), French and Tudor furniture, copper cooking utensils, toys and patchwork quilts. Then there is the contents of John Wellington Wells' Magic Emporium (*see* page 107).

Some of these items are craftsman-made and, where these craftsmen operate mail order, their addresses and details are in the List of Suppliers. Many items I have made or assembled myself. Dolls' house fairs are a fertile source of both finished work and DIY supplies. You should also explore mail order suppliers, craft shops, supermarkets and gift shops, particularly in seaside towns and beauty spots. These yield both furniture sets and useful resin items.

## WHITE-METAL ACCESSORIES

In $\frac{1}{12}$ scale, Hobby's and Phoenix carry a wide range of items for use as accessories. These include cooking pots, picture frames, kitchen equipment such as irons and bellows, clocks for various periods, telephones, music stands, musical instruments, ink wells, cameras, candelabra, Toby jugs, busts of Napoleon, guns, firearms, washboards, coat hangers, warming pans, toys, drying racks, fireguards, lamps, garden tools, walking sticks, record players and shop tills. Some of these items are shown in individual projects.

In smaller scales, specialist suppliers have their own range. Suppliers sell their own designs of tools, luggage and cooking stoves, including a complete Elizabethan kitchen and a Victorian lavatory. Besides their $\frac{1}{12}$ accessories, Phoenix have a number of items in their general and historical catalogue, including china, cutlery, weapons, picture frames, books, guns, gun dogs, food, candles, cooking utensils, kitchen jars and so on, which can be used for $\frac{1}{24}$ and $\frac{1}{32}$ scale.

A careful selection from the items sold for model soldier and war games enthusiasts will extend the range of small-scale accessories. Verlinden sell a beautifully detailed $\frac{1}{32}$ scale Victorian bathroom and kitchen. The kitchen set is complete, down to the grapes in a fruit bowl. Modern items such as Coca-Cola machines and barbecue furniture, not to mention news kiosks and shop fittings, are sometimes easier to obtain from model vehicle or train specialists. You can see examples of these on page 140. There are also a number of companies making small resin items, particularly radios, vacuum cleaners and modern household goods. Military figures and armour can, of course, be obtained both from war games and militaria suppliers. It is surprising what turns up.

The assembly method for most of these items, especially the smaller items, is relatively simple, and manufacturer's catalogues will help. Before painting or assembling, remove any small bits of flash or any unwanted marks from your item with a sharp modelling knife or a fine file. The item should be clean and free from grease before painting: you may need to wash it with water that contains a small quantity of washing-up liquid and a few drops of vinegar. All models paint better with priming: I spray batches with car undercoat. Some items, such as stoves and cooking utensils, are spray-painted with an appropriate coloured car paint. Use black for stoves and cast-iron cooking utensils, copper for copper utensils and gold for brass beds, some clocks, gilded furniture and personal items. Silver spray paint can also be useful. Resin items need to be very carefully prepared in the same way, and should always be given a good undercoating spray. Both acrylics and Humbrol enamel paints can be used. Very small items should be stuck to a piece of wood or card with masking tape, Blu-Tack or grip wax: this makes them easier to paint. Very fine sable brushes are lovely, but the best source of fine brushes is often the local model shop.

There are a number of skilled craftsmen working in wood. Even if you cannot turn wood, a number of small wooden accessories in a variety of scales are sold in hobby supermarkets. You should be able to find small milk churns, small butter churns, shapes suitable for kitchen boards and a range of wooden plates and bowls. You will also find that craft shops, florist's shops and cake decorating shops sometimes sell miniature baskets, hats and a selection of prams and cradles intended for christening cakes.

For components for making accessories, haberdashery departments and bead, jewellery and egg-craft suppliers have many items which can be used by the miniaturist, either as components or as ornaments. Gift shops, and I do not mean the sort that sell high grade porcelain, crystal and silverware, sell wire furniture in approximately $\frac{1}{12}$ scale and sometimes, if you are lucky, half scale, which improves with repainting, pencil sharpeners, all sorts of animals and various sets of imported furniture. There may be sets of china, vegetables, fruit and baskets of household accessories such as knitting and sewing. Cake decorating shops have a wide range of goods such as miniature birds, miniature figures and cradles and prams intended for christening cakes but useful for miniaturists.

Finally, there are a number of companies selling moulds that can be used to make or decorate accessories. Some of the vegetables and fruit made for the stall on page 103 is made from cold porcelain from a mould obtained from Cel Craft. Flowers are discussed in Chapter 7.

Bead suppliers sell beads which can be used as ornaments or vases, or as components in more complicated projects. The overlap between hobbies is well recognized, and if you wish to obtain a truly beautiful chandelier with real crystal beads, then Tee Pee Crafts will be able to assist you.

The subject of dolls' house accessories is such a complicated and fascinating one that a great many books have been published solely on this aspect of the hobby. There is a list of them in the Bibliography. This is not necessarily complete, as new books are regularly published.

# DESIGNING YOUR OWN ACCESSORIES

## RESEARCH

There is a golden rule when choosing, designing and making accessories for a project: never include any which are younger than the date you are portraying. If you must have a computer in your half scale study, then for authenticity you will need to include an occupant with a suit or jeans, polo shirt and trainers. Manufacturers of commercial dolls' houses of the sort sold for children tend to freeze their products in a particular period – nothing older or newer than that period is allowed to creep in. We all know that real life isn't like this. Even stately homes hang on to furniture and bits and pieces from earlier periods; after all, they may be valuable. The value of earlier generations' junk can be seen regularly in antique-hunting programmes and better still by visiting antique fairs and those which sell collectables and 'bygones'.

Regular readers of my column will know that I am a great devotee of armchair modelling. This is the process of mentally planning a miniature project which can take place anywhere, particularly in boring places like the dentist's and on the Tube. Sometimes, if one is lucky, it is possible to read helpful books whilst planning. Dover Books, in particular, sell and publish a huge range of facsimile period source books. The only difficulty with these is that they tend, with the exception of sketch books from great furniture makers such as Chippendale, to date from Victorian times. Even at a specialist fair it can be difficult to obtain much source material. I have, therefore, listed in the Bibliography books with examples of particular periods to help you create models from other periods. Where relevant I have indicated commercial sources of reasonably priced material which might be difficult for a kitchen table modeller to reproduce. To add enjoyment (I hope) to the process, where there are a series of historical novels about a period, or classics from that period which are readily available, I have mentioned these. Two general books which you will find helpful for the 1500s onwards are Peter Thornton, *The Domestic Interior 1620 to 1930* (Authentic Decor) and Sara Paston-Williams, *The Art of Dining – The History of Cooking and Eating* (The National Trust), which includes authentic recipes as well as lots of pictures of preparation and consumption.

Of course, mail order shopping requires a reliable postal system, but both America and the United Kingdom had wonderful mail order catalogues selling everything from patent medicines to toys, not to mention clothes, in the nineteenth century. Because these are illustrated by steel line engravings rather than the photographs now used in mail order catalogues, they are an excellent source for details of construction and material for would-be modellers. For example, page 1,196 in the *Army and Navy Catalogue* for 1907 shows ladies' dressing cases: Figure 46 is 'Morocco Leather 14' and contains two hairbrushes, clothes brush, tortoiseshell comb, soap jar, two scent bottles, powder jar, pomade jar, toothbrush roll, nail brush, paper knife, cutlery board, five instruments, scissors, folio, pen, pencil, ink bottle and a matchbox. It is described as silver and ivory fitted and cost £12 12s. Item 48, also a lady's dressing case, is a far more elaborate affair containing as it does seven silver-mounted bottles, two hairbrushes, a clothes brush, a velvet brush, a comb, glove stretcher, shoe lift, button hook, leather writing case, pen and pencil, ink bottle, matchbox, instrument board, three scissors, five instruments, tooth and nail brushes. It is also available in crocodile as well as the usual

Morocco leather. Comparing the two pictures shows that the No. 48 dressing case was well worth its £22 10s. Every item is decorated in elaborate chased silver work.

Inspiration for rather different model entertainment might come from the Entertainment Section which was described as being suitable for evening or juvenile parties, bazaars, concerts, balls, fêtes, galas, festivities, school treats, garden parties, barrack recreation rooms, institutes, and so on. You could have chosen from the society Pierrot Quartet, Wallah and Arho, the royal Durbah entertainers who specialized in something called the Indian Mango Mystery. Mr Sydney Gandy, the famous society ventriloquist and entertainer with his renowned figure 'Ebenezer Twiddlepump', a Punch and Judy show or Mr Robert Gilbert's marvellous troupe of acrobatic dogs. The performance was described as lasting for twenty-five to thirty minutes and a performing space 15ft wide and 10ft deep was required. This was described as being suitable for both in- and out-of-doors entertainment!

You may wish to reproduce violet mouthwash or white rose tooth powder. Suitable product labels, bottles and tins can be obtained from Valerie Claire. If you wish to reproduce a Victorian dentist or doctor, then you will find all the necessary surgical tools and dreadful-sounding patent medicines illustrated in the Army and Navy Catalogue. Again, Valerie Claire has a range of products and labels to help you.

I can't remember who it was who said that history would be more interesting if more attention had been given to the history of everyday life and less to the history of warfare. Future generations will, of course, have more than enough information about our own houses and their contents in the many interior design magazines and from television programmes and books. One of the difficulties about researching miniature houses is that much

of the social history information that is available is concerned with rather grand lifestyles. I admit to indulging in occasional grandeur myself. However, I usually make accommodation for quite ordinary people. Sometimes, the best source of period detail will be from a work of fiction. Charles Dickens' novels are full of minute detail, some of it distinctly macabre. Try reading *Bleak House* from a miniaturist's point of view. Jane Austen's detail is easily come by since the vogue for films of her work. I don't recommend Frankie Howerd's *Up Pompeii* for details of classical times but there are a series of videos of *I, Claudius* and *Claudius the God* which contain much accurately researched period detail. For a lower social scale, or at least a more impoverished one, try Lindsay Davis' *Falco* books.

You've selected your period. You know your characters life's history. So what do you put in their individual rooms, which accessories do you make and which do you buy? How much or how little do you put in a room to give authenticity? Late in life, the 19th century author and journalist, Clarence Cook, who was in fact an art critic, wrote a series of articles on home furnishings for a magazine called *Scribner's Monthly*. These articles were collected into book form and became *The House Beautiful*. This was first published in 1877, but has just been republished by Dover Books. I was particularly taken by the following paragraph which applies as much to miniatures as to full scale decorating:

Just let us comport our own desires and needs, and refuse to be governed by those of other people. And let us refuse to take what is offered to us, if it does not suit our needs or our purses, and learn not to fear being sent to Coventry for our refusal.

Like most Victorian work, this classic contains steel line engravings of enormous detail and great beauty. More usefully for the miniaturist, it deals with a middle-class home and with the choice of decorations and contents including the smallest and more trivial items. My favourite illustration is entitled 'Much in little space' on page 108. This contains a corner in an ordinary middle-class living room. In the little space are a small sofa, wall shelves containing no fewer than twelve assorted vases and other ornaments, a languid lady statue on a jardinière, two pot plants, a desk with more ornaments, books and an inkwell, a large stool with an Indian shawl over it and a small footstool, an Indian carpet, a Japanese scroll, a Chinoiserie plate and a picture. Everything, including details of wallpaper, panelling and dado moulding, can be clearly seen. The value of this book lies in its ability to explain, in a pleasantly idiosyncratic style, what might be included in various rooms. This is a book I tend to turn to when my mind has gone blank or when a house that I have lavished a great deal of time and attention on does not look lived-in, or appears stilted.

Some of the sections below overlap. There are no fixed rules. Some accessories I have dealt with in the particular project section for the model concerned.

# PERSONAL ACCESSORIES

In this category I would include the bits and pieces that, particularly, Victorian ladies tended to accumulate. Through the ages, ladies tended to treat their bedroom as their personal space. This was particularly true in medieval times when the solar or even the great bed with curtains was the only private space available, even to ladies of very high rank. The projects in this book include a Georgian bedroom, and a Victorian one.

Running water, as every child knows from school history lessons, was a relatively recent introduction in those eras – though perhaps out of deference to the Romans I should say it was a reintroduction! My bedrooms have facilities for washing. The Georgian bedroom, on page 129, has a period washstand with a jug and basin. The Victorian setting, on page 124, actually has a lady reclining in a hip bath complete with soap, sponge, back brush and suitable lather; she was purchased from Bustles and Beaus. The furniture is either adapted Taiwanese or made from a kit and decorated with découpage flowers. The paintwork has been distressed to make it look older. I have used fabric on the bedclothes and dressing table, and there is a needlepoint bedside rug on top of the Indian carpet, which was cut from a table mat I found in a charity shop. I find that ladies' rooms, particularly, look much more attractive if clothing and various hobbies are left out. In both $\frac{1}{2}$ and smaller scales, I make the clothing from cold porcelain since this is far easier to manipulate into the sort of little piles that are appropriate to go into small chests and chests-of-drawers, not to mention wardrobes. Both rooms include a chamber pot. These are relatively inexpensive to purchase, particularly if you buy a metal chamber pot and paint it. For half scale and smaller scales, a chamber pot is easily made from Fimo or cold porcelain.

Parasols and umbrellas add charm, and can be made from cold porcelain, Fimo or from fabric. If you have never made one before, a kit may be helpful. The Georgian room contains a sunshade made from cold porcelain: this is simply a circle of cold porcelain, frilled with a damask tool and then folded round a cocktail stick painted gold and given a handle from an appropriate bead. I added a few unpicked pieces of lampshade braid.

It is now possible to obtain half scale and smaller tea services and plates, as well as pots and jars. If you decide to make these for yourself, consider, particularly in small scales, making solid, non-functional versions.

Slippers and shoes give character to a project and can be used to indicate personality. A retired wing commander, who collects teapots and English porcelain and lives in a Dolls House Emporium Manor House, has rather battered bedroom slippers and a very elderly camel-hair dressing gown. The items have been soaked in cold tea to give them that well-loved and worn look. The impression I intended to give was that the wing commander preferred to spend his money on his hobbies than on himself. Concessions have also been made to the frailties of age by including various patent remedies.

Hats can also give an indication of the character of the occupant and add to a project. There are hats for Ascot, an ARP warden's hat, a highwayman's hat and, of course, hats for children. Of course, Sherlock Holmes needs a deerstalker. Sometimes it may be important to include an item of clothing that is no longer in common use such as a ruff, doublet and hose, a child's pinafore, or a liberty bodice. These can be made from fabric in ½ scale although I have to admit I usually use cold porcelain. In smaller scales, paper is more satisfactory, or cold porcelain again. Sometimes fabric can be rendered satisfactory for smaller scales by gluing it to tin foil, thus making it easier to handle.

Do not forget that even a spartan medieval castle would have had rushes on the floor and herbs to add some comfort. Bowls of pot pourri are not a recent development, and it is not difficult to produce minute pot pourri simply by opening a herbal tea bag; mixtures that include hibiscus are particularly good. You may need to add a few pinches from several different varieties. The advantage is that these also provide, at least for a little while, an authentic smell!

# TRAVELLING

The package holiday and the ease with which we travel the world today have made most of us blasé about travelling arrangements. As recently as Victorian times, however, travel was regarded as a very serious undertaking indeed. My *Army and Navy Catalogue* has vast sections of specialized luggage made of compressed cane, the best solid leather, patent steel, canvas of every sort and, of course, wood. Some of these, particularly those obviously intended for gentlemen travelling the world, are fitted out with what would now amount to a survival kit worthy of the starship *Enterprise*.

If you are interested in making luggage, it would be sensible to obtain a supply of junk mail with careful attention to be paid to the envelopes. These contain tiny printed paper designs on the inside of the envelopes which are extremely suitable for lining luggage.

Gentlemen, of course, had all sorts of sticks and canes in various shapes, with or without regimental crests. You may also wish to make a picnic basket or a fitted tea basket. An authentic period scene may very well have included evidence of sports such as hunting, shooting and fishing. I happily make walking sticks, umbrellas and a variety of sporting equipment, but model guns and fishing gear are relatively cheap and I therefore usually buy them as it is beyond my skills to make anything remotely authentic. Miniature food suppliers will provide practically any feathered or fur game for your hall or kitchen.

# WORK ROOMS

It is sometimes fun to have a butler's pantry/harness cleaning room, as I have done in the cabinet house on page 121. Miniature bridles, head collars and so on can be quite easily reproduced with thin leather, provided you have a catalogue to refer to and a supply of small buckles.

I also find useful a button-making tool sold by Holly Products. This enables me to make endless buttons from Fimo or cold porcelain. A few of these find their way into sewing baskets. Also useful is a stitch marker from the same source. It is not worth trying to make miniature tools: these are freely available commercially in a variety of scales. You may wish to make a toolbox or leather or canvas bag to put them in, and authenticity can be added by a pile of miniature planks and bits and pieces of moulding.

My Stockbroker Tudor scene includes a tool kit with a pile of precious wood and a few battered slates. These are included because my mother told hair-raising stories of her days as a fire watcher during the Second World War. For this project I was able to obtain miniature ration books and identity cards from the Cat's Whiskers.

# BEDROOMS

Apart from the personal paraphernalia of either sex which tends to be found in bedrooms, the average bedroom will need a variety of blankets, curtains, sheets, pillows and so on. These are quite easily made or obtained in ½ scale. Well-washed second-hand cotton or linen is best for sheets and this can sometimes be obtained from charity shops. Small shirt patterns make good mattress ticking. I use raw silks from the Silk Route for the hairier sort of medieval blanket which was woven at home. Various teachers attempted to teach me the rudiments of needlework: I think some of them would be horrified to discover that I use most of my carefully learnt skills in making curtains, bed covers and wall hangings for my houses.

In the photograph on page 137 you will see a blackwork bed cover worked on 24-count cross stitch material. The Quilt Shop on page 106 is in ½ scale and has, for the most part, been stocked with quilt kits from Hilda Burden, who has a wide range of small fabrics and can be found at dolls' house fairs. She also sells a few prints suitable for half scale. For smaller scales, you have a choice of printed paper, small rubber stamps, felt tips and the non-woven fabric that is used for baby wipes. Dry out the baby wipe and press it flat, then stamp or draw your design. If making a very small scale project, it is better to stick to very tiny squares of colour in a random but straight cottage-style pattern. These do look wonderful in shop settings or on tiny brass bedsteads made from kits sold by Phoenix.

Very grand and elaborate sets of bed covers and pillows can be made from cold porcelain if you use Cel Block as a basis for the bed and an embossing tool to make a quilted pattern. The elaborate round and heartshaped pattern cushions in my half scale hotel have been made from a press mould sold by Cel Craft. Murals and picture frames can be contrived from moulding, jewellery findings, egg-craft findings or from purchased metal frames. The best pictures are to be found in auctioneers' catalogues and in the yearbooks published by auctioneers such as Sothebys. These turn up at jumble sales and in discount bookshops.

# NURSERY

No miniaturist should miss a trip to the Bethnal Green Museum of Childhood which is world famous. I find my faithful *Army and Navy Catalogue* useful for indicating what sort of toys Victorian children had. Some of these are also suitable for an earlier childhood. You will see Georgian children's toys on page 131. When making toys from scratch, I tend to use either Constance Eileen King's *Encyclopaedia of Toys* or the *Army and Navy Catalogue*. Here are a few suggestions:

- Military costumes for boys. These were very common until relatively recently. Guns and swords can be obtained, together with all sorts of alarming ammunition from military model and war games suppliers.
- Building bricks. These can be made from offcuts of wood and packed in a box. They can also be made from Fimo or from cold porcelain, as can ninepins and skittles.
- Model soldiers. These are horribly expensive to buy ready-painted. I recommend that you purchase your own from a military model suppliers and invest in a good quality magnifying glass. Otherwise, follow the painting instructions for metal or plastic.
- Balls. These can be made from all kinds of modelling material, or a bead can be used.
- Boxes of animals and Noah's Ark. Make the Noah's Ark yourself from modelling material or from wood, and use farm animals or domestic animals from model railway suppliers.
- Puzzles. Labels for boxes of puzzles can be obtained from Valerie Claire Miniatures and other suppliers: you are most likely to find these at a dolls' house fair. There are also suppliers who specialize in authentic jigsaws.
- China sets for dolls. This is best achieved by using the next scale down: for $\frac{1}{2}$ scale use $\frac{1}{24}$ scale. Warwick have a range of white-metal toys which include accoutrements for dolls.
- Dolls and larger toy soldiers. These can be purchased as kits or made yourself.
- Dolls' houses. There is a project on dolls' houses and furniture on page 104.
- Cuddly animals. These can be made from pompoms which are sold in incredible tiny sizes or from felt or from velvet.
- Model horse and cart. Use small-scale railway items and paint them yourself.

- Clockwork trains. Small authentic replicas of clockwork trains can be obtained from Phoenix, or made from birthday cake candleholders.
- Kites. The ever-popular child's kite can be made from paper or silk on a wire frame. I use cake icing wire.
- Scientific toys. Scientific toys such as kaleidoscopes are difficult to reproduce so that they work. There is, however, a Dover book for cut-outs of various scientific toys.
- Child's dolls' prams. For child's dolls' prams or pushchairs in $\frac{1}{2}$ scale, use half scale. Railway suppliers occasionally sell model pushchairs or prams which are useful for smaller scales. The same applies to small-scale boats and cars.
- Stoves. For stoves, use small-scale for bigger scale toys.
- Rocking horses. These sometimes turn up made of resin in gift shops. A simple wooden rocking horse can be made from the press-out of a furniture kit of a nursery sold by Hobby's. Otherwise, adapt a plastic toy horse.

It is worth remembering that poor children had very few toys other than those made at home until Victorian times, and more wealthy children were often subjected to a nursery regime which concentrated more on education than on play, so you may wish to include a few improving books. You should certainly have an appropriate school clock, and tables and chairs for lessons.

# PARLOURS, STUDIES, LIBRARIES AND SITTING ROOMS

There are a vast range of fancy goods and accessories which can be included in any of these rooms, and easily made. Take, for example, paper. According to my book on etiquette, gentlemen used cream laid paper and ladies azure, with envelopes to match. Special notepaper was sold for use in the tropics. A death in the family required the use of mourning bordered notepaper, the border varying according to the identity and closeness of the relationship. Writing paper was sold generally in sheet form. Special paper was sold for a number of the professions; for example, clergymen had special sermons paper and the legal profession had a whole range of special sizes and grades of paper and envelopes. Tissue paper, butter paper and kitchen paper were a few of the other grades sold.

Knitting cases were in common use. Ink came in bottles or in powder form, and in the nineteenth century various commercial glues began to be sold. Pocket pencils are a fascinating subject in themselves: many were sold with a ring to enable them to be attached to a belt or fitted into a writing case. Most houses would have had a blotter and desk set which can be made from paper and leather. Pens and pencils can be contrived from wire, Fimo and especially cocktail sticks, which make very good pencils if suitably coloured. Metal typewriters can be obtained from the suppliers of white-metal castings, and there are many jewellery findings which make excellent inkstands and ink bottles.

Music and the paraphernalia that goes with home music making were a common sight in middle-class homes. Simpler instruments such as children's drums and tambourines may be contrived at home, and white-metal castings are sold of violins, trumpets, trombones and so on. Most dolls' house shops stock pianos and harps, starting with cheap imports and working up to the exquisite work of The Music Room. Sheet music can be readily obtained, although for smaller scales you may have to reduce it on a photocopier.

One of the first uses of reading and writing was to keep accounts. Double entry bookkeeping was invented in the Renaissance and it is appropriate in almost every house to have account books of some sort, and also writing desks. A writing slope looks good in a Victorian or Edwardian setting. Simple wooden boxes for writing slopes, jigsaw puzzles, building bricks and so on can be made from veneer or paper. By Victorian times, elaborate patent filing systems and safes were in common use, and bookcases came much earlier. With the penny post came letter scales. Use jewellery findings or white metal castings for elaborate stationery racks, blotting pads and so on. Books can be made from card, leather, wood and so on, or can be bought. Large houses often had a wooden post box and sometimes even an elaborate stationery cabinet.

Many dolls' house suppliers sell decanters and glasses. For authenticity, these can be stored in a simply-made wooden box or in a tantalus. Wooden boxes can also be used for tea caddies and tea cabinets.

Playing cards are an old amusement. These are obtainable in $\frac{1}{2}$ scale but for smaller scales there is little alternative to drawing your own or indicating play by a card box and scorer. Other games are more easy to obtain or to make. Chess sets exist in $\frac{1}{2}$ and half scale metal castings. Poker chips can be easily made from Fimo, as can cribbage and whist sets. The ladies of the house would, of course, have had both a writing case and a needlework case with thread cards, button cards and dress patterns. Bags and purses of all kinds give authenticity and a lived-in appearance to a house. A small silver box could be a card box.

Calendars can be purchased from dolls' house stationery suppliers and it is not difficult to write small letters or to contrive a stamp or odds and ends box. A ball of string and sealing wax are normal equipment too. Paperweights can be made from modelling material or from beads. A paper knife requires a jewellery finding and a piece of foil from a takeaway container. Clocks are readily available in metal castings, or more sophisticated versions can be purchased from specialist suppliers if you want your clock to work.

Sweet dishes and *bonbonnières* as well as snuff boxes are fun to make from modelling material and jewellery findings. Victorian households had a whole variety of newspaper racks and bookstands. Bookstands have been in existence in the form of a bible box for many years. If you need a small-scale bible box, these can be obtained from Phoenix.

From Georgian times, young ladies were encouraged to attain accomplishments and no parlour, schoolroom or even lady's bedroom is complete without sketchbooks, paints and albums of various sorts. In particular, the Victorians had a passion for so-called fancywork, which embraced lace making, shell work, wax fruit and flowers, découpage and paper filigree work. The list is endless. There are books on these various hobbies listed in the Bibliography.

Wax fruit can be emulated from modelling material, as can wax flowers. Shell work requires diligent searching of your local beach, or a shell supplier. Collections of minerals can also be created, as can collections of coral. If you are not able to afford and cannot muster the necessary skills to make miniature tapestry work, consider cutting out something suitable from a needlework catalogue or magazine. You could reduce it, if necessary, by photocopying and inserting this work in a suitable frame. I like doing miniature needlework and, as you can see from the projects on pages 106 and 108, some of my dolls knit, sew and even do patchwork.

I plan to include a loom, spinning wheels and carding combs in a medieval castle. For small photograph frames or fire screens, try either a jewellery supplier or an egg-craft supplier. Photographs can be obtained from suppliers of dolls' house stationery, or specialists will reduce full-size photographs for you. Another popular decoration was engravings and etchings, of both fine art and scantily clad ladies. Reproductions of these can be bought at dolls' house fairs or cut out from clippings. Artists' materials can be made from modelling materials and fitted into suitable wooden boxes. Dolls' house easels and sketch books can be purchased in varying qualities, or you can make your own. Do remember the fondness for chalks and modelling materials. A clay figure adds authenticity to a miniature studio. It is not difficult to draw out a small ruler and geometrical tools on wood and mark them using Indian ink.

The Victorians were fond of flowers and pot plants, and these are covered in the section on gardening, as are suitable floral arrangements for other ages. Right through history women have gathered herbs and sweet-smelling flowers to perfume their homes and themselves, and to disguise less pleasant smells. In small scales, rubberized horsehair and railway foliage are best.

Smoking tobacco has been popular in this country since James VI of Scotland and I of England ranted at great length about the evils of tobacco. White clay pipes are appropriate in Tudor scenes and in Victorian times wooden pipes in increasingly elaborate forms became popular. Cigars are also appropriate to a Victorian or Edwardian scene. Cigarette holders became popular in the 1920s and were usually made of amber, ivory, ebony or jade, as well as some precious metals. Contrary to popular belief, they were used by both sexes. A nice touch for an upper-class 1920s scene is a silver cigarette box with the pastel-coloured cigarettes so popular with fashionable ladies at the time. Pipe tobacco was, until relatively recently, kept in small pouches and sold by the ounce. Appropriate labels for tobacco and all sorts of smokers' goods can be obtained from label suppliers.

Alcoholic refreshment is covered in some detail in the houses and the hotel on page 139–144. At first, sweets and biscuits were made at home for the most part, although professional bakers and sweet sellers have been recorded in Rome and other large ancient cities. The large-scale production of sweets, chocolate, crystallized fruit and so on was the product of the Industrial Revolution. Glacé fruit, which always looks pretty in a dolls' house setting, should be displayed in round or square wooden boxes. The fruit is made from modelling medium with salt for sugar and varnished to make it shine. The boxes are made from offcuts of wood. Chocolates, fudge and fruit creams are made from Fimo and shown either in authentic boxes and labels or, as was common in Victorian times, in baskets or flower-covered and novelty boxes (*see* the Sweet and Cakes on page 109). The *Army and Navy Catalogue* lists a huge number of sweets of various sorts. All of these can, to a greater or lesser extent, be reproduced in modelling material. The best ½ scale sweet jars come, surprisingly enough, from opticians. Contact lenses are sold in small glass jars which even have a very satisfactory plastic lid. These look just like old-fashioned sweet jars.

Biscuits seem to have been largely made at home until the First World War, though a few commercial brands were sold for export or alleged to have some sort of health-giving quality for children or invalids. Labels for packets of biscuits and for biscuit tins can be obtained from dolls' house stationers. Huntley and Palmers, Peek Frean and Co. and MacFarlane Lang and Co. were flourishing. No Victorian or later grocers is complete without biscuit tins and possibly even a glass-fronted special stand for the sale of commercially made biscuits.

Cakes, scones, tea cakes, muffins and crumpets are easily made from modelling material. These would usually have been made at home. As you can see from the cakes in the cake shop on page 109 I sometimes manage to stick to my diet by making whatever cake it is that I really would enjoy at that moment in miniature. This strategy does not always work and is no way guaranteed!

Decorative tea sets and coffee services need to be appropriate to the period. Teacups, for example, have not always had handles. If you want to reproduce tea bowls, you may have to file off the handles from white metal castings before painting. Making crockery from modelling material is enjoyable, but practice is required to produce satisfactory results. For a beginner I would recommend the metal sets sold by Warwick, Phoenix and Hobby's. Delightful crockery can also be purchased from specialist suppliers.

Miniature living rooms are a matter of personal taste. It is quite valid not to wish to include dolls if these offend. However, a great deal of atmosphere can be added to a house by including family pets. Again, white-metal castings exist in a huge range of sizes down to $\frac{1}{144}$ scale if your eyes can stand it or you can make your own from modelling material. Another sometimes ignored source is toy shops. My children and grandchildren have satisfied an early collecting bug by the purchase of small, plastic cats, dogs, guinea pigs, birds, hedgehogs and so on. These can be a little lurid when purchased but, providing you do not intend to resell them, it is acceptable to repaint or even flock them for greater authenticity. If you require something really special, then the dolls' house press carry advertisements from artists who will undertake commissions.

Finally, most rooms improve by leaving small items of clothing about, such as a pair of slippers or a shawl.

# 10

# Pottery Houses

*Mouseville.*

## MOUSEVILLE – PUMPKIN VILLAGE

This project has been christened 'Mouseville' by my family. The big pumpkin house been joined by a smaller pumpkin and friend, two sorts of squash (these are what we Brits call vegetable marrows or gourds), a radish bandstand, a mushroom house and a pile of fruit to make a kind of adventure playground for little mice. My mice have all sorts of civic and domestic

attractions to keep them amused, ranging from a privy to the left of the picture to a statue of Mouseville's founder in tasteful bronze, and a street market. The street market stalls came from the Harrow Model Shop; they are made of resin.

There is an antique stall, a toy stall, a flower stall and, of course, a vegetable stall. These are wonderfully detailed. The antique stall has mirrors, marble busts, crocks, shoes, books, teapots, ornaments, a pipe and even a copper plate and an oil lamp. The vegetable stall has all sorts of clearly defined vegetables including a pumpkin and some beautifully modelled cabbages and cauliflowers. On the toy stall you will find a magic set, a rocking horse, a dolls' house (of course), a clown doll, teddies and a cricket bat, not to mention a toy boat. Hanging from the side of the stall are a number of kites. The flower stall is so pretty that it has a nasty habit of disappearing into my friends' handbags – need I say more! It is funny how the nicest of ladies sometimes combine kleptomania with dolls' houses.

If you want a similar street market, a mail order source of market stalls is JoJay Crafts. You will find all the different varieties, including a hot-chestnut seller and an ice cream stall, in their current catalogue. Phoenix also sell white-metal kits in smaller scales. Hobby ceramic studios are a fertile source of unusual and reasonably priced bits and pieces including houses. The market leaders are American and they supply plaster of Paris moulds. The basic set-up is as follows.

For those of you who do not want to go to the trouble and expense of firing your own pottery, studios like Two Hoots provide a casting and firing service. The model is made by pouring liquid clay into the plaster of Paris mould, leaving it in the mould for long enough for a skin about the thickness of a 50p coin to form. The rest of the clay is then poured out to use for something else. At this stage the model is referred to as green, that is, unfired. Ceramic buffs talk about greenware (unfired) and bisque (fired but not yet painted or glazed). If you had dreadful experiences at school or evening classes of wobbly ashtrays and lumpy models, then try a day or even an evening at a hobby ceramics studio. The American and British companies supply both glazes and non-fired finishes in a huge range of colours and textures in nice little pots just right for miniature work. The main companies in the UK are Duncan, Gare and Ceramichrome.

# QUARTER SCALE HOUSES

This project is a village made of hobby ceramic houses. I saw a $\frac{1}{12}$ Tudor complex at a racecourse fair and dreamed of something similar until – fortunately – my husband

*Quarter scale ceramic house front* (top) *and back* (bottom).

pointed out that as this piece was taller then he is and wider than I am, something on a much smaller scale would be more appropriate.

There is a long tradition of miniature villages in America, particularly for Christmas, made with all sorts of materials. I have used a ceramic base from a Christmas village to put my first two little houses on; these came from Two Hoots in Guildford. I particularly like the crooked house on the right of the picture. To convert them from ornaments to dolls' houses, at the greenware stage I brushed cooking oil on the area that I wanted to cut out and cut a section out of the back wall. The oil lubricates the knife and prevents unplanned cracks. The greenware was then cleaned and fired, and then painted with Ceramichrome paints and antiqued to bring out the detail. I then dry-brushed the woodwork and tiles and sprayed the houses with clear varnish.

The technique is the same for both houses. Both have balsa-wood floors. The garden is made from model railway landscape materials with another statue from Anna Lamour. The smallest size of paper flowers are used with two pot plants from a Phoenix kit. The tiny pond is Super Seal varnish poured into one of Carol Mann's pots. I have used the smallest paper leaves and flowers tinted with pink fibre tip to make a water lily. The garden furniture is from Just-in-Case.

# DRACULA AND A PAINTED LADY

The adventures of Count Dracula, a former resident of Transylvania, are supposed to be based upon the escapades of a real baddie, Vlad the Impaler. Unless one is more familiar with Martian culture than human culture, it is impossible to escape the reworking of the original legend, and

*Count Dracula's residence.*

particularly variations on Bram Stoker's play. The latest of these has been a film and then, of course, if you need further research on vampires, there are the novels written by Ann Rice.

Despite the fact that Dracula has nasty personal habits and a rather limited diet, there is a kind of awful glamour attached to the character and to his various hangers-on. He tends to live in various picturesque dwellings which, even if not ruined, are usually unorthodox, if not chaotic. There is plenty of room for artistic licence and camp Victoriana. A melodramatic project of this sort is the perfect antidote to a succession of thatched cottages set in pretty gardens.

One of the purposes of this project is to show you how to set a $\frac{1}{24}$ scale house in a scene. Let's start, therefore, with the basics of building the scenery. I should stress that the majority of the materials which I refer to below can be obtained from railway model suppliers or, in the case of more generalized products, from DIY chains all over the country.

Scenery will greatly enhance your project. My banks, mountains, rocks and foundations of houses, not to mention Count D's personal vault, all need foundations on which to fix trees, scrubs, plants, rocks and so on. I start with a flat base board, usually MDF or flooring grade chipboard. This project uses newspaper as a support for bandage soaked in plaster of Paris.

If you were creating a very large scene with several houses, as is perfectly possible in $\frac{1}{24}$ scale, though rather unwieldy in $\frac{1}{12}$ scale, you would probably need to use a series of card or polystyrene supports and formers. Count D's main support is the room box which I have incorporated as his vault. My main support is pink financial papers made damp – the ink does not run so much as the tabloids' – and screwed up into appropriately formed balls and cliffs. These have been laid against the room box in what I hope is a fairly artistic fashion. The resulting structure can be covered in a number of ways. The cheapest of these would be a sort of papier mâché made by soaking strips of newsprint or computer printout in wallpaper paste. I prefer to use a proprietary product which consists of plaster-impregnated bandage, such as Mod-Roc or a similar product. Mod-Roc strips need to be cut up and then soaked in cold water for a moment or two and laid across the top of the crumpled newspaper.

Because my scene is relatively small, at least in model railway terms, the cost of plaster-impregnated bandage has not been prohibitive. Those of you on a budget or with much larger ideas may wish to use pieces of soft old cloth such as T-shirt, or even ordinary shirts soaked in Polyfilla.

I cannot stress too strongly that plaster of Paris in this form dries incredibly quickly. This is not a project which can be done by instalments at the scenery building stage. Mod-Roc ceases to be workable in fine hot weather in about four minutes. Lay the Mod-Roc over whatever former you are using and use the working time to remove any undesired creases with your fingers, or with a damp, fairly stiff paintbrush. Excess plaster of Paris can be poured on to the scene. Never, ever, pour plaster of Paris down a sink or drain: it sets hard, and I am sure I do not need to point out the potential inconvenience. You should keep unused Mod-Roc away from sources of water as it is 'deliquescent', that is, it absorbs water.

By the time that your project is dry, the result will be quite rigid and surprisingly tough. However, you should bear in mind that if the model is going to be moved around for exhibition purposes, it will probably be better to use either crunched up chicken wire, florist's wire, thick polystyrene or even wood as a support for the Mod-Roc. You will see from the photograph that I have tried to set the house into its scenery by taking the scenery right up to the sides of the house. I also added a few trees at this stage because it is easier to embed the trees into the plaster while it is wet. Many garden shrubs are suitable for this purpose, once dried. I use pieces of forsythia for big trees and spiraea for smaller trees.

When the Mod-Roc had dried, I spray-painted it with a selection of car paint sprays which included basic grey undercoat and then dribs and drabs of brown, beige and green. Just plain green or brown would have looked artificial. You could have used a variety of paints other than spray car paints: acrylics, poster paints and emulsion are all suitable.

A huge variety of materials are sold for miniature landscaping. The most useful is a very fine dust-like material called Scatter Material. It is prudent to apply this with a good-quality tacky glue and to use at least two layers, otherwise the slightest damage by handling will be conspicuous. I do not need to remind you that for the initial layer any cheap fine brown material which is not attractive to cruising mice can be used. The real scrooges among you will find that dried tea leaves are pretty satisfactory as well as being pleasantly scented, depending on the variety that you use.

Once the first layer of Scatter Material is dry you can shake this off so that the loose material can be re-used. Re-coat the area with tacky glue and now use better-quality Scatter Material. Brands vary but a good selection can usually be obtained at any large model railway show. You will find if you look at your garden that scenery is hardly ever consistently one colour, and it is therefore sensible to mix green, brown or whatever mixtures you can get hold of. Don't forget to save the excess.

For actual rock faces, I used Tetrion or Polyfilla. It is better to use several thin coats and to mix some tacky glue with the product as plain Polyfilla or Tetrion has a nasty tendency to crack. I know that rocks crack anyway but you really don't need to have your own miniature landslide. You will find the process of buildings rocks and scenery so they look more or less natural is much assisted by using photographs, and that a photograph is the only way to achieve a realistic cliff. This is another occasion when the application of a variety of dry-brushed paint colours in natural shades of brown, green and grey can add character and authenticity.

To add further detail, you can work additional patches of vegetation by dabbing more glue on and using foam ground cover. The textured scrub is made by using a kind of reindeer moss, much beloved of miniature flower arrangers. It comes in a huge variety of colours and any small pieces should be saved for miniature pot plants and flower arrangements. The darker green shades are absolutely wonderful for miniature Christmas scenes.

The Dracula residence is in two parts. These began life as a bisque house from a Ceramichrome mould and a $\frac{1}{2}$ scale room box. The house was cast in a complex block-and-case mould. If you do not wish to do your own casting and firing, then it is possible to obtain both greenware and bisque through hobby ceramic suppliers.

Once the house has been fettled and fired, it is time to start painting. This for me is the fun bit. I start by giving the house a spray undercoat of car paint. You can use either white or grey, depending on how much gloom fits in with your personal taste. This is then antiqued with brown or grey transparent paint. Do remember that rags and paper towels which have been soaked in spirit for antiquing are potentially flammable and should be disposed of sensibly. When the model has been antiqued, you can then dry-brush the tiles and brickwork with a variety of colours according to your fancy. I have used pinks, greys and browns from the Ceramichrome and Duncan ranges. These are all acrylics which are extremely versatile. You can use them on any surface from fabric to glass. They also have the advantage of being opaque, which means that mistakes can be painted over.

The delicate gingerbread trim on this house was painted with acrylic paint and

*Dracula's house painted to be the Painted Lady.*

the detail was picked out with a gold fibre-tipped pen. White detail has been added using a wood-painting pen. These pens can be obtained from many dolls' house suppliers and are extremely useful for fine detail, particularly if you are not too comfortable using a fine sable brush.

Once the house was painted, I sprayed it with satin varnish to add depth to the colour and protect my work. The inside of the house can be painted in the same way.

I used a kit to build the room box for the marble effect vault, The finished box was then sprayed with grey car paint. I used a natural sponge to sponge white acrylic on the dry car paint.

I used a selection of rubber stamps in this project. The most exciting of these is designed to be used to obtain a variety of stone finishes. It is a cube with three sides which does quite excellent stone, marble and something that looks remarkably like cement, which you may need for a road surface. This stamp is referred to as a 'texture cube'. Most rubber-stamp suppliers can obtain them. They are made by Stampendous Incorporated. I used a permanent ink from a multi-coloured (dark colours) stamp pad. You may be interested to know that, as well as using the texture cube to stamp ink or paint, it can be used to create texture in Fimo or other modelling materials. The only limitation is that the modelling material should be the sort that is clean and does not stick in crevices. I also used rubber stamps to create the doors and shutters in the vault. Much as I love modelling, I find that repeating very detailed drawings is quite difficult and even sometimes tedious, especially when they keep going wrong. These rubber stamps are ideal for this purpose and can be obtained from most stamp suppliers. You will usually find that there is something that can be used for gargoyles or carvings in most stamp ranges, too.

If you want raised detail, then the sensible way to do this with a stamp is to emboss the design. To do this whilst your stamped impression is still wet, you sprinkle embossing powder over it, shake the surplus off and then heat the paper with a hot air blower or a steam iron in accordance with directions supplied with the embossing powder. You have a choice of colours: gold and silver are effective, as are black and transparent. Transparent will simply emboss the colour of the ink which you have used. Black looks wonderfully creepy for a Hallowe'en scene. For ease of use and density of colour, I would stamp your door and shutter images on satin finish white card of the sort often used for cake and cosmetic boxes. The mid-floor and partition in the crypt has been constructed out of plastic building materials, painted in the same way as the rest of the crypt.

I had a teenage craze for leatherwork. This was not terribly successful as hobbies go: it didn't take me very long to discover that there is a limited market for key fobs and so on among my family. Large pieces of leather are expensive and Marks & Spencer make better handbags than I do. However, the punch and the little stamps which come with it are marvellous for detailing Fimo and, even with a good hard whack, soft wood panelling in models.

The furniture has been created by spray painting a plastic set in black car paint and picking out the details with gold pen. A variation on gold pen is lustre wax. This comes in a range of colours and allows for attractive mixed finishes. The slime moss and general grunge is achieved with paint, bits of old railway scatter and even a little dust from the vacuum cleaner bag.

Count D and his Lady are plastic figures from car boot sales, repainted and dressed in tissue paper and net. The cats, ghosts, pumpkins and so on are sequins, and the wreaths were made from telephone wire. The Knight in Armour is from a souvenir shop. A plastic figure was converted into a white and grey lady – the bride who was jilted. This is done with scraps of net and chiffon. The skull is a bead and the two little ghosts come from a Kinder egg.

I am sorry that I cannot share with you the totally chilling effect of fitting a clip light inside the main house. The same house looks quite different if painted in pretty colours (see page 89).

# 11

# Papier Mâché Houses

## TEAPOTS, JUGS AND POTS

Papier mâché is an increasingly popular craft. It was first popular in Victorian times, being used for a variety of decorative projects and even for small furniture. You can either make your own shapes using the methods set out at pages 27 to 28 or begin by purchasing the reasonably priced shapes to be found in craft shops and supermarkets.

My village started with some gnome figures bought at a souvenir shop in Cornwall. I then needed somewhere for these characters to live. At first I thought a pumpkin house would do but there were going

*Pots, jugs and teapots.*

*Pots, jugs and teapots details.*

to be obvious problems with the doorways. I used a mixture of bought and prepared papier mâché shapes.

The two teapots are treated in different ways. The black pot has been painted with a proprietary iron paint and then treated with a patination that produces instant rust. Inside, the walls have been painted white and then dirtied down with a transparent wash of burnt sienna. The blue and white Cornish ware teapot has a yellow interior. The outside is painted in bands of blue and white which has then been sprayed with high gloss varnish to look like glazed Cornish ware. If you have difficulty in painting straight lines, use masking tape to give a straight edge.

The cracked jug shape is painted white inside with a floor of 'earth' and small wooden tiles. The outside is painted white and then sponged with various shades of blue. The jug was then treated with a two-part crackle varnish finish which explains its presence on the rubbish tip.

92

Next door to the jug is a flowerpot. This is one of the easiest shapes for a beginner to make since flowerpots are not valuable and they tend to be regularly shaped, as they are made in moulds which are designed to be easily released. The outside is painted terracotta that is then dirtied with brown and green paint. Inside it is painted white with a shower stall made out of a shampoo bottle top and part of those little bottles obtained from hotel bedrooms. The steps are made with polyfiller and wooden tiles which have been stained with oak stain.

The boot at the back of the scene came from HobbyCraft. The boot, and indeed the teapots, had to have apertures cut out of the side. This is easily done with a pair of scissors. The inside of the boot is white. The outside was spray-painted brown and then treated with boot polish and a little textured paint for mud. The sole of the boot was created with cast iron paint. I then used wax polish and finally random slashes of varnish to give the impression of cracking leather. You could use crackle varnish.

Such furniture as there is is re-polished Taiwan dolls' house furniture, except for the kitchen which is a resin set. I placed the various completed items on a piece of board and played about with their positioning, in some cases propping them with pieces of flower arrangers' fungus or, if the prop was invisible, small pieces of polystyrene tile. When I was satisfied, these were glued into place.

The basis of the vegetation is a piece of railway grass which I have sponged with well-watered brown and yellow paint. The bumpy steps are made from the dried fungus sold to flower arrangers and I have added pieces of railway moss and coloured sponge. Remember that all scenery is better, i.e. more durable, if fixed with a proprietary cement sold for scenery, such as Scattergrip.

At the front of the scene, to add a little life and movement, is a small pie tin with a couple of flower arrangers' insects. Portraying water is an obsession with modellers and various sorts of plastic and resin are pressed into service. You can even, as with my Roman garden, use the real thing. The simplest way to show water is to cut a piece of clear plastic – of the sort sold for dolls' house window glazing – into an irregular shape to fit the desired space. This is painted with matt paints on one side (use acrylics, not oils) in a mixture of dark greens, blacks and browns. The top surface has been made to look like water by painting it with tacky glue which, of course, dries clear. This ripples the surface of the pond and makes it look more lifelike. To add realism, arrange some railway vegetation over the edge of the pond to hide the join and dot a few small pieces of fungus and driftwood at the edge as well.

It really isn't obligatory to have gnomes in this sort of setting. You could just as well create a mouse village or provide a project for a child who is reading or watching *The Borrowers* or *The Wombles*.

The background to this scene is made from a selection of plants from my own garden. If you do not have a garden, a wide selection of dried flowers and vegetation is sold in hobby supermarkets, and florists also sometimes sell them.

# INDIAN LAKE SCENE

Découpage is a Victorian hobby which is enjoying a revival. It can transform uninteresting containers into eye-catching houses. I have used two different basic shapes of boxes which can be readily obtained from craft suppliers. It is important to seal the box or house which you are going to decorate first. The papier mâché boxes which I used in this project have been undercoated with emulsion paint left over from painting my full size house. This both seals and fills the papier mâché.

*Indian lake.*

Découpage experts recommend coating both sides of gift wrapping paper or photocopies which you intend to use with Shellac. This protects the paper from adhesive and varnish, and also strengths it. It has the useful side effect of making detailed cutting easier, too. If you use Shellac, which is the most readily available sealer for this purpose, then you will need to clean your brush with methylated spirits. Both boxes have had windows cut with a Stanley knife.

The vaguely oriental pavilions have been decorated in two colour schemes, terracotta and lavender. The gold lattice trim is sold as découpage material. I recommend this as useful material for all small-scale modellers, as there is no easy and cheap alternative way of producing so much detail. It can be sprayed with acrylic paint if you don't want gold, and cuts easily with a pair of scissors.

Other decorations are glitter glue, which is available in sets of six colours, sequins and stickers. Readers with young children will know that stickers are a current craze, and these have potential for modellers: pictures of flowers and teddy bears can be used in nurseries or as pictures, and the way over-the-top sparkly three-dimensional hologram stickers can be used for more exotic projects, or even for a mock mosaic floor in my pink pavilion.

The lake is a mirror with a pretty frame from a craft fair. I bought the two small elephants at the first Hove fair that I attended. The potted plants are made from modelling clay and railway vegetation.

# —12—

# Cold Porcelain Projects

## THE PARTY HOUSE

The basic house for this project was constructed amazingly quickly from a kit imported from Spain by Hobby's. The kit is so simple to assemble that there are no written instructions, just pictures on the box. It slots together, although it is

prudent to use good quality wood glue for reinforcement.

I wanted to make a setting in which all scales commonly in use in the dolls' house world could be combined and in which I could use a variety of fantasy figures which I had either collected or wanted to make. The guest list includes Cinderella and her Prince, a number of musicians playing

*Party house.*

*Musicians from party house.*

medieval and earlier musical instruments, clowns, wizards, a Snow Queen, various little figures collected over my travels round the country on behalf of my clients, Father Christmas, Good Queen Bess, the Green Man to represent life, and a skeleton for death. Smaller guests included fairies, leprechauns and gnomes. In the end it seemed like a good idea to have some sort of supervising presence to organize the catering and throw out the drunks, particularly since so many of the guests brought their pet dragons, owls and other beasties with them. A fairy godmother with a slightly anxious expression fulfils the role of hostess and organizer.

I completed the kit in accordance to the instructions on the box. The inside of the house was painted gold upstairs using a good quality bright gold paint from a folk-art paint supplier. Downstairs was painted deep red with a gold ceiling. Skirting boards, dados and plasterwork are made from gold découpage paper cut to shape and cold porcelain strip. The mural at the back of the top room is a design taken from a book of China designs. The design is called 'Indian Tree'. Instead of just photocopying or drawing this, I traced the design in white pencil on to a piece of Pergamano parchment and then embossed and coloured it. The design is framed with découpage paper. Upstairs a set of cheap furniture has been sprayed in a pale creamy pink which has been distressed with white lime wax and then gilded. I used a small pink floral fabric to imitate petit point. The cabinet holds a collection of cranberry glass from Glasscraft.

Party goodies are predominantly puddings and these are made from Fimo in the same way as the cakes and patisseries sold by the cake shop on page 109. The food is served on paper plates which have been decorated with gold and silver gel pens. Downstairs is furnished with a elaborately carved plastic set which was originally in quite typical colours of bright blue, bright lilac and bright tangerine. I sprayed all the pieces with red oxide car undercoat and then with gold car spray. This was further highlighted with a variety of gold waxes. Chairs and stools were recovered with a small print reminiscent of medieval tapestry. The flambeaux or candle holders were part of this plastic set and have been sprayed with red oxide and then gold paint with candle detail added with acrylics.

# ¹⁄₁₂ SCALE COLD PORCELAIN FIGURES

All the cold porcelain figures were made by either of two basic methods. The simpler method involves a cone of Cel Block which is covered with cold porcelain. The figures which are made in this way are Miss Haversham, the Snow Queen, the Wizard and the Green Man. These are fantasy figures designed to stand sturdily – once completed, they are not flexible. This is a party scene and their purpose is to add glitter and colour. For speed and ease I have used face moulds to create the face masks. The Green Man and the Wizard are made with Holly Product's smallest size of clown mask. The Snow Queen is made from a Cel Craft cutting sheet which contains eight different faces, and Miss Haversham is made from Holly Craft's female mask mould. The method is similar for all figures. Variations in heads and accessories are dealt with below.

## THE GREEN MAN

The basic large cones sold by Cel Crafts come in packets of three. One of these is covered with finely rolled green paste. Roll out the paste on a non-stick board with a sugar roller and cut to size to cover the cone. Paint the cone with white glue and then wrap it in the green paste and trim to fit, tucking the paste under the base and paying particular attention to the join. Leave to one side to dry. Mix up apricot-sized balls of pale green, pale brown, dark green and mid-green paste. Roll each individual colour ball out and cut out with the middle size of carnation cutter. Divide the sections of carnation into four and frill extensively with a needle tool or silk veining tool. Attach the resulting leaf

*The Green Man.*

*Wizard and Snow Queen.*

head-dress are made with more leaf shapes made with the carnation cutter. Any gaps can be covered by additional leaf shapes and I have also added sparkle by using leaf-shaped sequins. The finished figure was allowed to dry overnight. Check for any shrinkage and, if necessary, fill with a little coloured cold porcelain paste mixed with a little additional water. I painted the face with pale green acrylic which was then painted over with green pearlized paint. The figure was then dry brushed with gold, bronze and green acrylic paint.

## THE WIZARD

The Wizard is made in the same way as the Green Man. His cloak has been textured with a smocking tool. It is made from black paste which has been highlighted with pewter-coloured metallic wax. The Wizard's beard and hair have been made from spare black paste left over from the cloak which has been dry-brushed white and grey. His hat is simply a cone of rolled-out black paste. The under-robe and the hat have been highlighted with mauve pearlized paint. I textured the robe by using the top of a shampoo bottle which had an interesting design on it. You could use a leather punch or embossing tools.

## THE SNOW QUEEN

The Snow Queen is made on a basic cone of paste coloured very pale blue which is then painted with blue pearlized paint. Her face is made from white paste tinted with white gouache and then painted with white pearlized paint. Her hands are made from individual very finely rolled sausage shapes of paste. Each is fixed to a basic mitten shape and the finger are marked with the rounded end of a toothpick. The dress has been trimmed with sequins, lampshade braid and snowflake shapes but from lace. Again sequins have been used.

shapes in a spiral round the cone with white glue, leaving space to fit the arms and the head. Allow to dry. Make the arms by making a cone of green paste. Attach these cones of paste to the figure with white glue. Hands are made by winding strips of paste which have been rolled out with a smocking tool over flower wire.

The round wire strips of paste should be wound round a basic hand-shaped armature made from florists' wire. The head is made from the basic mask made by pushing a ball of clay into the clown mould and fixing it over a cotton ball. The beard and

## MISS HAVERSHAM

This figure was inspired by some beautiful but worn lace purchased from Hilda Burden which had handkerchief points. The base for the wedding dress is a cone covered with deep cream paste. The face was made with the same mould as the Snow Queen. Lace was then arranged over the cone shape and a separate train with further lace attached to the back of the figure. The sleeves were covered with lace as well, with the lace being deliberately distressed.

*Miss Haversham.*

Miss Haversham's hair is made from cat fur which has been teased with a comb. Her veil was made by joining two pieces of lace with fabric glue. The head-dress is made from white cake-icing wire, frayed lampshade braid and very tatty dried flowers. Some more tatty dried flowers have been incorporated with the frayed lampshade braid into a battered bouquet. Miss Haversham's cello is a Christmas decoration with the integral cherub removed.

The second method for making figures is to use a cake icing mould, also used for the Neptune project on page 149. Cold porcelain cannot be used to model solid figures and for that reason, although solid legs and arms can be made, you will need to fill the bodies with tin foil or Cel Block as an armature. Female figures with long skirts such as Good Queen Bess, the lady musician in the butterfly head-dress and the green dress, Cleopatra and the gypsy are all made as variations on a basic theme. Their skirts are cold porcelain draped over a basic armature of tin foil. Remember that cold porcelain dries hard. The cold porcelain is wrapped over tin foil which has been wrapped over a small block of Cel Block.

### CINDERELLA

Cinderella's skirt is the most elaborate. It was made by covering the basic skirt shape with white paste. A body shape was then built up on to this skirt shape, again from white porcelain, and a front panel cut for the dress. Sleeves and train were also cut from the same white paste. I textured the skirt and train and the front panel with embossing tools and put a frill of silver grey paste at the bottom of the dress. The arms were made by pressing flesh-coloured paste into one half of the arm mould, which was sufficient for this scale. The arms were then stuck to the main assembly and petal-shaped sleeves added. The rest of

*Cinderella.*

## QUEEN BESS

Queen Bess is made in much the same way as Cinderella, save that she carries a small nosegay of flowers and has a ruff made with paste cut with a carnation cutter, and a string of pearls around her neck. Her hat is no more than a blob of black paste frilled at the edges, with two or three egg-crafter's jewels. The fringing at the bottom of her dress has been unpicked from lampshade braid, but small fringing can be obtained from Hilda Burden or The Dollshouse Draper.

## EGYPTIAN LADY

The Egyptian lady is a simple column of Cel Block covered with pure white paste coloured with white gouache. Her gold collar is made from paste textured with an embossing tool and decorated with small pieces of sequins, and very narrow gold braid. Her dress is textured with a smocking tool and her hair is a simple Egyptian-style wig made from black paste. She wears simple gold sandals which have been painted on to her feet. These are made from the cake-icer's mould, but they have been cut down to ankle level.

## BUTTERFLY LADY

The lady with the butterfly head-dress is made from the same sugar craft mould. Her body and face are made from the cake icing mould save that the face is made from one of Hollycraft ladies' moulds which has much more definite features. The elaborate hairstyle was made by covering a U-shape of foil stuck to the back of her head and arranging ringlets to conceal the joins. A very fine circular piece of white paste was then draped over the head as the last stage. Before draping, edge this paste with a stitch marker. The instruments were made by In Some Small Way.

Cinderella's costume is a mixture of pink guipure lace and silver lampshade braid. Her head was made with a Hollycraft mould and the mask has been fitted over a cotton ball. I did not bother to back the cotton ball, as I wished to make an elaborately ringleted hairdo. This has been made by covering the back of the head with yellow paste textured with a smocking tool. I then made individual ringlets by winding paste which had been pushed through a garlic press round a cocktail stick. This has been dry-brushed with gold paint and finished off with a string of pearls.

## GYPSY PRINCESS

The princess wears a white paste blouse. Her generously endowed figure is created by two half spheres of tinfoil glued to an appropriately shaped piece of Cel Block. Her skirt is made from textured green paste trimmed with black lace and her bodice is made as shown in the photograph. Two gold rings have been glued as suitable earrings. These are jump rings from a jewellery supplier. The same techniques are used for Columbine.

## OTHER FIGURES

Male figures with legs, such as Prince Charming, Pierrot and the Egyptian gentleman, are made from a cake-icing mould. Prince Charming has been dressed in breeches and tunic cut from cold porcelain and textured with a smocking tool, and his doublet is made from plain paste cut from the pattern with a ruff cut from white paste with a carnation cutter and then heavily frilled. The stockings are painted and small shoes are made by shaping blobs of black

paste and then placing small ovals stamped with a flower design using an embossing tool. The hat is made from rolled-out paste moulded over a cough sweet bubble pack, textured and trimmed with braid to match the braid stuck to his suit.

Mother Bear has a head made from Cel Craft's teddy bear mould and is made in the same way as Cinderella, save that she wears an apron and a mob cap which is a circle of frilled paste draped over a small silver paper ball which has been squashed flat on to the bear's already dried head.

The Celtic Princess, the Druids, the elves and the nasty monster with the teeth come from a fantasy chess set mould sold by Doc Holliday, an American company whose products are imported into this country by Hobby's, Ceramicraft and others. Father Christmas is from a Gare mould. I used acrylic paints with clear varnish and lots of glitter glue for these figures. The collection of fairies with parasols and mushrooms and the small gnome clutching a bunch of toadstools were bought whilst on holiday, from a seaside gift shop.

*Gypsy Princess and Mother Bear.*

(Above) *Pierrot and Columbine.*

*Assorted figures.*

Brigitte Heywood made the beautiful Wizard of Fire Mountain, to which I added a little red glass dragon. She also made the dragon sitting on the tapestry chair talking to Cinderella. The two clowns are made from pipe cleaners. The fairies are made from cold porcelain from a Cel Craft fairy mould, and their wings from a butterfly wing mould from the same source. Their hair is made from unravelled Binka braid.

The borrowers are the smallest size of railway figure and the coach that they have arrived in is a pencil sharpener. Two dogs of Fu are from a war games kit which can still sometimes be obtained from Verlinden suppliers. For instructions to make flowers from cold porcelain (*see* page 63). Tiny jewelled crowns, like the Snow Queen's, can be obtained, as can replicas of the Crown Jewels, from souvenir shops in London and bigger cities.

# ¹⁄₁₂ Scale Shops

## THE VEGETABLE SHOP

This is a basic stall purchased from Prime Properties. I painted it in shades of green and covered the base with stone paper and the front of the stall with green velvet ribbon which is pre-wired. This seems only to appear at Christmas time in both dark green and red, but it is so useful for miniature projects that it is worth laying in a stock. The wire edging means that it can be easily arranged.

I varnished the painted stall to make it easy to clean. The lettering has been done with a Dover Books Clip-Art package. I called it 'Ceres' because I wanted the stall to sell plants, flowers, vegetables and whole foods. Most miniaturists seem to start with food made in either Fimo or other modelling compounds. Fimo vegetables are easy to make: most vegetables are sausages or spheres in shape, and these can be given character by additional paint or texturing.

To add variety, I have also used an Amaco push-mould and cold porcelain from Cel Crafts to make lots of sweetcorn, carrots, aubergines, Italian tomatoes, peas in the pod, beetroot and Swiss chard. Broccoli is

*Vegetable stall.*

*Vegetable stall proprietor.*

made by slicing off the tops of the turnips and adding small pyramids of paste textured with an old but clean toothbrush. The globe artichokes are also made from cold porcelain: a sphere is created by covering a foil ball with cold porcelain and then sticking on small cold porcelain leaves which are still pliable and shaping them to give the characteristic structure. When creating vegetables, it is absolutely crucial to have at least a good photograph, if not a sample of the real thing, in front of you.

Containers for the stall were small baskets bought commercially. As well as dolls' house suppliers, try basket shops and florists. I also made small boxes from card and from scraps of wood. The proprietor is made from a Holly Products clown mould which comes with figure-making directions. His hair has been made by sieving cold porcelain coloured black and then, once it has been fixed to his head, dry-brushing this. His corduroy trousers were made from pieces of textured green cold porcelain which have been distressed and antiqued with acrylic

paint. The denim waistcoat has buttons which are made with a button stick and the glasses have been made from a brass etching. Sacks can be easily made from cotton. Do remember that white can be overwhelming in small scale; cold tea makes a good dye.

The sweets and nuts are small groceries like cous-cous or poppy seeds, or cut-up pieces of polystyrene. They are kept in little glass jars which I get from my optician.

# A DOLLS' HOUSE SHOP

One of the best sources of very small houses in ¹⁄₁₄₄ scale to use as dolls' houses for dolls' house dolls is the railway modelling suppliers. A variety of historically accurate card kits, which are very reasonably priced, can be obtained from Freestone Model Accessories. I was particularly taken with 'Fiddlers' Green', which is a series printed on postcards which you can cut out and make up; some of these are shown in the photograph. Individual houses cost just a few pennies.

My house kits in the shop are made from plastic kits sold by the same supplier, from whom I was also to obtain appropriately sized brick and tile paper. The Tudor and Victorian houses at the front of the photograph came from the Lincoln Dolls' House Shop. The two unpainted Tudor-style thatched houses are from Shire Buildings.

My ¹⁄₂ scale shop is a kit intended for children from Hobby's. The brickwork is brick paper which I always tone down with varnish tinted with burnt umber. The Victorian stonework is cut from embossed wallpaper and then painted with stone-coloured paint from the National Trust paint range sample. The red paintwork has been done with Eating Room Red from the same range. The tiles in the porch are made from cold porcelain stamped with rubber stamps, painted with suitable Victorian colours and then antiqued. Flooring can be obtained from Hobby's; the mosaic floor downstairs is a 'freebie' from an interior design magazine.

The furniture is made from two flat-pack kits which seem to be obtainable from most dolls' house suppliers. The furniture has been stained with dark oak stain and then finished with wood seal, as I find that wood seal alone is usually too light in small scale. Very small furniture can also be obtained from dolls' house suppliers, where it is sold as toys for half scale dolls.

My shopkeeper or craftsman is a resin figure repainted. The till is a pencil sharpener and was the only bright feature of a very long hearing in a very cold court in Wales.

*Dolls' house shop exterior.*

# THE QUILT SHOP

This is a labour of love. During my professional life I have done a lot of travelling and small needlework projects are much easier to carry and to do on trains and in court corridors than something larger and more elaborate. Most of the stock consists of pre-printed quilt designs obtained from Hilda Burden and worked in the traditional way through a layer of fabric, a layer of wadding and then a backing fabric. There is a huge choice of designs. It is also possible to buy kits to make pieced quilts. I have used one of these to make bundles of 'fat quarters'. My patterns, templates, cotton and so on come from Valerie Claire kits or have been made up from cuttings from quilting magazines. The patchwork rug is my own design and is made in cross stitch on Aida fabric. It is so simple that I have not bothered to reproduce a chart here. The quilt shop occupies the top of a single-fronted Sid Cooke shop.

# THE MAGIC SHOP

The bottom half of the Sid Cooke shop is The Magic Shop. The whole kit is well made and astonishingly easy to assemble. The Magic Shop is the place where I put all sorts of strange and wonderful items. The interior has been painted deep blue and over-painted with gold glitter glue. Shop fittings are made from a flat-pack kit painted gold, then crackle glazed and over-painted with turquoise. Carvings are made from cold porcelain. A pair of ivory dragons, a soapstone cat and various other interesting-looking beads came from bead shops. The jars and bags of spells and the Grimoire and spell books, as well as the small square boxes, are made from Fimo by me. Glassware was bought at dolls' house fairs or from Valerie Claire.

*Quilt shop interior.*

*Magic shop.*

The crystal ball is a clear glass marble balanced in a wooden turned dish. The cauldron, witches' hats, ghosts and owls are simple push mouldings. Two silver boxes are unpainted Warwick miniatures and the smaller boxes are bead spacers with diamanté and Fimo marble balls pressed in to form a lid. The Genie and, indeed, his bottle are made from Fimo in much the same way as the cold porcelain figures. Poison jars, skulls, Cornish pixies and a tiny Egyptian cartouche are presents from my family. Valerie Claire sells suitable jars and you can see these in the window.

There are also assorted small monsters and I can honestly say I don't know where my grandchildren get these, but they are all welcome. The shopfront itself has been embellished with a variety of stickers and Day-Glo stars. The tiny blue plaque was bought at Hove and bears the following verse:

> Life is mostly froth and bubble
> Two things stand like stone
> Kindness in another's trouble
> Courage in one's own

J. W. Wells' shopfront was done with rub-on lettering. The zodiac on his front door came from the Bead Shop in Covent Garden, London.

# DRESS SHOP

Both this shop and the establishment of Mr Charles Mould are in a double-fronted Sid Cooke shell kit. The dress shop fittings were made by Apollo Miniatures and the sewing machine is a Chrysnbon plastic kit. The Dolls House Emporium sells various suitable bits and pieces if you don't want to make your own scissors and dressmakers' dummies, but by far and away the best source of ¹/₁₂ scale and other miniature paperwork such as labels, fabric bolts and so on is Valerie Claire Miniatures. They also sell kits for parasols, tape measures, scissors, needlework baskets, coat hangers, corset patterns, dressmaking patterns, button cards, hat stands, and so on.

The lace hats are made by stiffening small doilies and attaching them to a shampoo bottle with a rubber band, then leaving them to dry. The grander Edwardian hats on the sofa are made, as are their matching gloves and bags, from cold porcelain. Once you start looking, there is an endless supply of suitable moulds for hats. My favourites are the blister packs for cough sweets, shampoo bottles, deodorant caps and marbles.

The carpet for this shop is painted and was made from a kit by d.ann Ruff. I bought the peg lady and the dresses, which are not made from cold porcelain, at a fair and, now cannot trace the name of the supplier. If anyone out there can help, please write to me care of the Publisher.

## CAKE, SWEETS AND BREAD

Charles Mould's Emporium is stocked with a variety of cakes, biscuits, sweets, pies and cheese, and tea and coffee. In other words, it sells all the things that I am trying to give up! Glass jars in suitable sizes can be obtained from various dolls' house suppliers, and also from opticians who store contact lenses in them. The sweets and groceries are small seed beads, poppy seeds, hundreds and thousands, silver and gold cake decorating balls, made from chopped up polyfoam in pink and white, and Fimo.

*Dress shop interior.*

*Grocer's shop.*

One of the delights of Fimo, and other polymer blending clays, is that they can be rolled in the same way as the sugar that was used to make original boiled sweets and ice lollies. This means that you can made a large cane of lollipop design and then roll it on a board with your hand until it gets smaller and smaller. You then chop slices off and bake in accordance with the manufacturer's instructions.

Cakes can be easily made from Fimo. For bigger cakes I use a mixture of cold porcelain, wood and acrylic paint with the occasional dash of bath sealant as cream. Bath sealant works well in ¹⁄₁₂ scale but is too coarse in texture for use in smaller scales. In ¹⁄₁₂ scale, beads and small pre-cooked balls of Fimo can be used as fruit filling for pies. I glaze these with tinted varnish or glass paint. Glass paint makes excellent fruit glaze, or even the sauce at the bottom of an ice cream sundae. I made various shapes of loaves and buns from salt dough, adding poppy seeds, pepper and even tiny pieces of pre-cooked Fimo for colour, and other bread ingredients. The better-quality pastries in the window of the shop were bought.

The wooden boxes, sacks and shop fittings were made from a kit purchased from Hobby's; the ice box came from a plastic kit which has been so distressed and battered by me that the original suppliers may not wish to be associated with it. The glass and wood counter and the cake display unit are from Ann Underwood; these are sold as whitewood and I have painted and varnished them. I made the chocolate Easter eggs and boxes of chocolates from chocolate-coloured Fimo shapes which are presented in small baskets made from coiled Fimo. Toffees, fondants and other luxury sweets are made in the same way. Most of the dolls' house magazines from time to time carry cut-outs for groceries and biscuits which you should find easy to use.

*China shop.*                                        (Below) *Country-style shop.*

# 14

# Half Scale Shops

My three double room boxes are from a well known DIY furnishing store. Most mail order craft suppliers also sell them. I have divided them in half with a fake floor made from Polyboard and Contact sticky plastic. They have slide-out glass which has been removed for photographing purposes.

## CHINA SHOP

My first room box is a china room decorated in lemon yellow to provide a foil for a collection of blue and white china. The problems here were where to obtain small-scale supplies of china or china substitutes, and what to use for half scale paper plates. So far as I am aware, and I would love to hear news to the contrary, nobody sells half scale paper plates. I make mine out of flat white card, using a plastic icing stencil, although a compass or any suitably sized bottle cap can be used to draw circles. For my blue and white patterns I used $\frac{1}{12}$ willow pattern saucer transfers obtainable from Phoenix suppliers and small cut-outs of blue and white china. I find tile catalogues and interior decorating materials a particularly fertile source of these small motifs.

The large open vases on the floor and on the barrel-shaped seats are Phoenix castings spray-painted white with transfers cut to size. Transfers (also known as decals) can also be obtained from hobby ceramic suppliers. If you have trouble in persuading your transfer to curve round a small shape, aircraft and railway modelling suppliers sell a proprietary product called Micro Sol for softening transfers which is most useful for small curved surfaces. The Chinese barrel seats are painted wooden barrels. Some of the craft supermarkets sell suitable barrels, milk churns and butter churns in packs of ten. It is worth remembering that the smallest size of blue and white china in $\frac{1}{12}$ or $\frac{1}{16}$ scale is sometimes suitable as a large piece in half scale. The set of three covered vases is an example. These are sold as tea and coffee canisters for $\frac{1}{12}$ scale.

The furniture, including the two fireplaces, is from a Taiwan set and, like everything else made from resin or plastic, these can be repainted if you first prime them with car undercoat. I wanted a blue and white china room, so have repainted the fireplaces and the cache-pots so that they match my colour scheme. If you find using a small brush difficult, it is possible to purchase roller-ball pens with indelible blue ink; these are useful for blue and white china projects.

There have been a number of famous china rooms in dolls' houses which are now in public collections, particularly in Amsterdam. Postcards and wrapping paper from museums sometimes provide useful motifs. The beautiful real vases are from Poppe Goet Miniaturen at the Alexandra Palace show, and Veronique Cornish made the birds.

## COUNTRY-STYLE SHOP

My next room box is a country-style display. One of the other items which is easily obtained in $\frac{1}{12}$ scale, but almost impossible to obtain in half scale, is patchwork kits. To help those of you who want quilts, I suggest the following.

Dolls' house suppliers carry a range of paper quilts which look very realistic, particularly since the paper they are made from is embossed. You can make your own quilts by selecting a very small patchwork-style cotton print (as in the photograph) and sticking these with tacky glue to tinfoil. This process ensures that the quilt can be convincingly draped and folded. The foil backing method helps to drape very small-scale curtains and is also useful in all scales if you want to display items folded, in a cupboard or drawer. It is probably the only way of creating a convincing lingerie collection in any scale of dolls' house lady's bedroom.

I found a great many helpful pictures of suitably styled American folk art in the catalogue called *New England Direct*, telephone number 01527 577111. They have delightful full-size pictures with appropriate mottoes. The two that appealed to me were 'Cats are children only with fur' and 'Grandmas/ Grandpas are just recycled little girls/little boys'. *New England Direct* do not sell miniatures but they have a large range of books on American country-style and crafts and the catalogue itself is full of potential clippings for your chinaware and picture gallery.

For authentic country colours, I paint furniture with paints intended for hobby ceramics. My shop furnishings come from Apollo Miniatures and have been stained with stain from a Trent Workshop wood finishing kit. The printed posters, button cards, shop signs and other paper ephemera come from Valerie Claire Miniatures. These are much easier to cut if you use a pair of découpage scissors.

## THE GENERAL STORE

The rolls of materials and piles of sheets and pillow cases were made by me. I used extra-small prints sold for dolls' house patchwork for the dress materials and wound these round thin card. The sheets and pillow cases are folded round a core of foil to keep them flat and are made from Vylene and dried-out clean (!) baby wipes. Valerie Claire sells a variety of tins, bottles, groceries and labels. My newspapers and magazines are cut from advertisements for new subscriptions. The iron goods such as kettles, saucepans and oil lamps are made from Phoenix kits. I used half scale moulding remnants for shelves. Baskets and barrels are from a craft supermarket.

My shopkeeper is a garden scale railway figure.

(Above) *Shopkeeper detail.*
(Left) *General store.*

# 15

# Quarter Scale Shops

The property for this project is commercial premises with living accommodation above. The original house shell was made by Tom's Miniatures and came from the Newbury Fair. It has large shop premises with an ornate Victorian-style facia. The ground floor is divided by a passageway, but the two downstairs premises are separate. I made the traditional shop into a general store and the other premises into a dressmakers and milliners. I cannot wait to use the hat boxes, which come from a set from Valerie Claire.

Upstairs is a workroom and living accommodation for the lady artisan. Quarter scale models fit in with railway supplies intended for O gauge, which is one of the most popular scales for dioramas and model railways. This means that there are copious commercial supplies of appropriate figures, vegetation, fences, walls and, of course, trains.

*Rear view of a quarter scale grocer's with two quarter scale Tudor houses. (The front view is shown overleaf.)*

Fully clothed people are available in O gauge and 1/43rd, dressed to suit various periods from Victoria to modern. Cheaper figures come packed like sweets, suitable for a crowd. These are made of the sort of plastic that can be easily trimmed with nail scissors or a modelling knife and are usually sold as they come out of the mould in packs of as many as twenty figures. One of the major advantages of quarter scale is that the commercial supplies for figures, furniture and so on are very cheap.

Milliput is sold in several grades including Superfine. Its advantage for very small-scale figures is that it adheres to plastic figures. Milliput is prepared for use by mixing the two component materials together until thoroughly blended, in accordance

with the directions on the packet. I use a variety of cake icing tools and old dental tools to model with. Dental tools are particularly useful for small-scale modelling: they turn up in model suppliers' catalogues, tool shops, model shops and car boot sales.

You will need a sharp needle-shaped tool, a rounded ball-headed tool and something with a spatula shape to smooth your work with. The spatula-shaped tool can be used to smooth the Milliput and also to scrape off any unnecessary lumps or bumps. Milliput has quite a long working time and is air drying. It should be that a small figure is dried enough if left overnight to dry.

Once your figure is complete you can refine it by using sandpaper, glass paper, wet or dry, or a good-quality file. I prefer tungsten carbide files such as Perma-Grit as these maintain their efficiency and can be used for all sorts of materials. If they become dirty and clogged up they can be cleaned with paint stripper: use the gel sort that is painted on.

Painting small figures is an art form in itself, and you are bound to improve with practice. The basic steps are as follows.

*Front view of a quarter scale grocer's with two quarter scale Tudor houses.*

Spray a very thin undercoat of grey and white car paint or modellers' primer. You will find it helps to hold the figure steady with double-sided tape, plasticine or Blu-Tack. Do not use gripwax, as the greasy residue can spoil paint adhesion. Once you have base-coated your figure, you will need to use magnifying glasses; if, like me, you normally wear bi-focals, you may find a magnifying visor makes for better painting.

After I have painted the first coat of clothes, flesh area and hair, I antique with a thin wash of antique medium applied very gently with a soft brush and remove equally gently with a piece of T-shirt material. Additional highlights can then be added by dry-brushing with a stiff brush. With very small figures there is no point in individually painting facial features, except possibly for a clown or for musical actresses. This can be done, but it is only satisfactory with very strong magnifying equipment. You can add interest by gluing on suitably sized lace or trim or by making additions such as hats or trade tools.

# 16

# Period Projects

## SHERLOCK HOLMES

The room box concerned, which stands on elegant little feet, was made by Bryan Frost and purchased at Newbury. It has a removable lid and a removable glass front. The design is a great boon since it makes decorating, a difficult task in ½₄ scale room boxes, much easier.

This scene is a special for a Sherlock Holmes fan. It involved lining the box which I have previously stained and polished with a removable lining of suitable Victorian wallpaper. The figures for Holmes and Watson are from Phoenix. My enjoyment of Sherlock Holmes stories was fuelled by my father who used to read the originals to us as children. In consequence I really resent Watson being shown as a bumbling clot. My Dr Watson is smartly dressed and reading *The Times* in his comfortable chair. Holmes is still clad in his dressing gown, playing the violin. These figures are ½₂ scale and are part of the current Phoenix range. Holmes and Watson come with a neat little stand.

However, I wanted to include Mrs Hudson as well. To do this I kit-bashed a Phoenix governess figure and included a table laid for tea, a fireplace and various other small

*Sherlock Holmes close-up.*

furnishings from the Phoenix range. I also put a false floor in so that I could pin the figures in place.

Metal furniture is always better spray-painted. Start with dark red primer, then use a dark brown gloss from a car paint supplier. You may wish to mask out the leather bits and the chair with small bits of masking tape. Suitable colours for the chair would be red or bottle green; bottle green also came in handy for the potted palm and the aspidistra. My carpet is dress fabric, wrong side out.

Watson wears a dark grey suit with a discreet fancy waistcoat. He has a receding hairline and a small moustache. Victorian gentlemen used hair dressing or pomade and this accounts for the large number of sleek black-haired gentlemen. I made Holmes clean shaven with a rich red dressing gown. Both gentlemen have black shoes. Mrs Hudson wears a deep blue ensemble with white lace trim. As she is the housekeeper, I have not added an apron although, if you feel strongly about this, one could be added with Milliput.

The fireplace is from a kit, as are the fire irons. I cut pictures from fine art magazines and Christmas card catalogues; the kind of magazines which purports to serve interior decoration for country homes is a useful source of cuttings. The food is made from cold porcelain – I have confined myself to an iced cake and some bread and butter.

# EGYPT

My collection of cuttings and scraps yielded a splendid Egyptian wall painting. I used four Shire books: *Egyptian Painting and Relief*, *Egyptian Models and Scenes*, *Egyptian Temples* and *Tutankhamun's Egypt*.

*Ancient Egypt.*

My husband hoards Styrofoam as a land-scaping material for his model railway, so I already had some experience of both the virtues and vices of this cheap and common material. Sticking Styrofoam is a matter of trial and error. Even glues which are expressly designed for plastic, like Metpack, melt my lovely white masonry. In this project, I used Aleene's thick tacky glue which sticks plastics and also non-matching items like wood to plastic and metal to plastic.

My shopping list for this project was five roughly square pieces of polystyrene, some sand-coloured masonry paint or spray fleck paint, black matt car spray, a packet of Milliput, various Egyptian wallpaper cuttings, mostly from the Sunday newspapers, and from my box of might-come-in-useful-scrap, I took eight plastic wedding cake pillars, some very chipped candle sticks and an assortment of plastic animals and figures the children had discarded over the years. I also have a biscuit tin with buttons, bits and jewellery findings. From this, I took small beads in appropriately Egyptian colours and one or two jewellery findings which I used squashed flat. I also used a sheet of cardboard.

The first step was to look for pictures of suitable temples. Bereft of their pillars, these seemed mostly to come in a basic square shape which was impressive by reason only of its size. Detail seems to have been added by columns and statues. Some of you will remember the exhibition of Tutankhamun's treasures.

One of the attractions for me in this project was to go over the top with the gold paint and gilding wax. I started by building the basic room box from squares and one oblong base piece of styrofoam. The roof is just a piece of card with a square of styrofoam glued on top. I sprayed this with suitable paint. You could use leftovers of masonry paint, the object being to achieve the texture of stone. The two gold statues of Rameses-never-was and Rameses-not-quite

were made from plastic figures to which Milliput clothes and jewellery finding jewels were added. These were then stuck to a piece of wood which was in turn cut to fit the top of a wedding cake pillar. I sprayed these with gold car paint. These figures are roughly $\frac{1}{2}$ scale so look massive besides half scale figures. If you have seen John Romar's programmes on the television you cannot fail to have been overwhelmed with the massive scale of ancient public buildings. The animal statues were suitable toy animals picked for their loose connection with Egyptian mythology. These were sprayed with matt black car paint and then highlighted with gold lustre wax. The gold bird statue canopic jars with scarabs and masks of Pharaoh at the foot of the statues were cast or modelled in Milliput and treated in the same way as the animal statues.

At this stage of the construction, one of next door's little darlings said that 'Egyptians have mummies don't they?' Back to the drawing board! A trip to the British Museum showed they are roughly human scale and often stand on some sort of special sarcophagus or tomb. To be fair to next door's little darlings they did supply the two deodorant tops which I finally used. I modelled the mummies in Milliput after measuring for $\frac{1}{24}$ scale, painted them black, rubbed them with gold wax as before and finished the whole item off with turquoise, terracotta and gold beads, and some disassembled earrings.

Massive granite pillars presented problems until I turned my scrap box upside down and suddenly discovered a set of vile candlesticks which I distressed with enthusiasm and Milliput, and stuck to either end of the cardboard tubes. These were sprayed with stone-coloured paint for texture and then with car paint. The trick with these was to spray the car paint randomly. I was looking for the appearance of worn sandstone, not more glossy gold.

Plastic figures (sold by garden railway suppliers) can be easily assembled with Metpack glue. Give them a base coat with car under-coat and then paint them with acrylics. The lady is dressed with two silk flower petals and a gold wire girdle; her jewellery is just gold felt tip. The priest has a kitchen towel kilt and a Christmas ribbon head-dress. I stuck two Egyptian-style clippings to a Cassidy kit

to complete the furnishing, and applied a collection of cuttings to the walls.

My main difficulty with this project is that the cats are fascinated by it, especially my husband's elderly Burmese who was always telling us that he was a cat god in a previous incarnation!

*Ancient Egypt.*

(Below) *Ancient Egypt detail.*

My alternative Egyptian room box filling has an historical theme. As historical figures go, Egypt is a convenient period both to model and for fancy dress. Cleopatra clad in lots of jewellery and not so many clothes is shown on a marble floor with marble walls. Again, the model is from Phoenix and includes a splendid couch and a little stool to hold the basket of figs. I sprayed the couch black and then highlighted the carving with gold; the stool was treated in the same way. Cleopatra was first undercoated with white undercoat and then painted as follows:

Flesh – flesh colour
Dress – white and antiqued pale coffee colour
Hair – black
Jewellery – gold achieved by applying gold wax very lightly to an undercoat of dark red

Asp – black-highlighted silver
Bracelets and sandals – gold

It is essential to use a very fine brush for details on a figure like this.

The basket of figs was sprayed brown highlighted with a little copper wax and the figs painted with green and mauve acrylic.

The statues and various religious items come from a mould sold by the British Museum which can be used either for Fimo or cold porcelain.

# CABINET HOUSES

I always wanted a cabinet house, ever since as a little girl my father took me to the museums in Amsterdam. These trips were a special treat and we spent many happy

*Cabinet house front.*

hours looking at the cabinet houses and planning our own together with all the items that would need to be included. I found a suitable cabinet at Masterpiece Miniatures in Marazion in Cornwall, an eighteenth-century cupboard that had already lost its decorative statues and its doors – who knows what sort of base it had. However, thanks to preliminary work by James Hickling, to whom I shall always be grateful, the woodworm was treated and suitable floors had already been put in.

There are six smaller rooms, two large rooms and three drawers. In addition, there is a large area above and I have plans to extend downwards with a suitable stand. As you can see, the cabinet is beautifully carved and I have highlighted the carving with Venetian gold wax from Liberon. For the moment, the cabinet house has temporary doors. These are made from board covered with classically patterned fabric and embossed paper. For the middle door I have made gold mouldings of cherubs and other suitable twiddly bits with cold porcelain. The moulds used for this are from cake decorating moulds. The side doors have repainted Christmas decorations as centre features, as the house is decorated for Christmas.

The inside of the cupboard was in beautiful condition and in many of the rooms I have simply used this as panelling. Throughout this house, having been held down and bullied shamelessly by a young friend who works for one of the leading London auction houses, paper and flooring have been temporarily fixed in a manner to ensure that my modern additions can be removed without damage to the structure of the cabinet.

The hall has been furnished with a set of sideboard table and chairs that have been stripped down and French polished. The marble alcoves came from The Merry Gourmet, and I made the two little statues from an extremely useful Egyptian mould obtainable from the British Museum. It is always worth looking at museum cata-

*Cabinet house hall.*

logues: quite apart from the cut-outs, the children's section often contains items of use to the miniaturist in the way of rubber stamps or moulds for Fimo. The Egyptian cat and the treasure chest both came from Nick Forder and have been dirtied up with a dilute wash of acrylic paint and then waxed so that they have that authentic 'Grand Tour' souvenir look. All of the people in the hall are resin figures that have been repainted to a greater or lesser extent.

The parcels on the table have been cut from a string of Christmas decorations. My Christmas wreaths are made very simply by twirling a string of dolls' house foliage round some florists' wire and, in turn, round my finger. Baubles have been added by using dots of glitter glue and I used a bow-maker to make tiny silk ribbons from red silk ribbon. The filigree Nativity ornament which would be useful in a half scale house came from JoJay Crafts.

The next room up is a butler's pantry. The butler, poor man, has a cupboard full of cleaning stuff, mostly made from Fimo with labels from Valerie Claire, and cloths, boxes and so on made by me. A furniture set has been distressed. I have a completely unique distressing system for furniture: I just leave it in my studio (the garden shed) for two or three months, and the combination of damp and pottery dust usually does the rest. This is only recommended if you want real Victorian/Dickensian dirt. The fireplace is a plaster of Paris sale special painted red and then marble-ized with gold, grey and black paint. The spinning wheel waiting to be fixed is a pencil sharpener – I have only myself to blame for dropping this on the way home! The shoes came from Maple Street. The silverware is bought, save for the big candelabra which is a Hobby's white-metal casting dirtied up with paint and Liberon wax so that it looks like tarnished silver. The eperne is made with egg-crafting pieces from Tee Pee Crafts. There are two delightful little specials made by James Hickling: a set of duelling pistols and a tool set.

The bedroom upstairs contains a fireplace bought from Halcyon whilst on holiday in Devon, as was the pretty scrap screen. The bedroom suite is another Taiwan set, this time stripped down to look like pine. The stool and plant stand are from a press-out bedroom set which I have painted to look like French country furniture. They actually go with the wardrobe in the other bedroom. The two figures are standard resin characters repainted in prettier colours, and they are lolling around on home-made quilts. I made the jug and basin in my own kiln, and the light and its shade are composed from beads and pretty ribbons stuck on top of a large bell cap. The carpet is made from some stuff called Crazy Foam, intended for children, which most craft suppliers now seem to stock; it makes wonderful dolls' house carpets.

Upstairs in the middle of the house is a sitting room. This is my special room in which a group of Gilbert and Sullivan enthusiasts have met to sing *The Mikado*. The suite is

*Cabinet house butler's pantry.*

*Cabinet house bedroom.*

*Cabinet house sitting room.*

made up from re-polished Taiwan pieces which have been re-upholstered in deep red velvet. The bas-relief over the fireplace is from Anna Lamour. The fire screen contains a Russian icon bought at Hove. The bronze ladies are egg-craft supplies sprayed with red undercoat and two sorts of gold metallic car spray; the same combination has been used for picture frames. The pictures are cut from auctioneers' catalogues. The two vases and dogs on the mantelpiece came from Past and Present; the two little Staffordshire cats were bought at a fair and the birds in the dome are by Sadie Jocelyn. I found the round house in the dolls' house shop in Veryan, Cornwall. The carpet is by Moorhen Miniatures. The crockery is metal castings, fettled and painted by me. The various scones, cakes, etc have been purchased from time to time at Hove and other EMF fairs.

Downstairs in the dining room a family wedding is in the course of celebration. A Taiwan furniture kit has been re-polished and re-upholstered with red velvet. Two Taiwan tables have been joined together to make a big one. On this is displayed a dinner service from Victoria Fasken. The glassware is by Leo Pulley. The Christmas decorations are made from bits and pieces from a well-known DIY chain; the two little Christmas trees on gold stands came from Tesco and once had peppermint creams in them. The champagne is in an urn which was originally a second from Hove. This has been filled and painted gold, and the ice is made from a smashed car windscreen. The figures are resin characters from dolls' house shops everywhere repainted appropriately. The bridal couple are a wedding cake topper made from resin. These come in any colour so long as it's white and to paint them you will need to give them a good undercoat with car undercoat spray. There are two cold porcelain figures in this scene: the housemaid and a Victorian lady in a grand green dress. Both of these are made from a cake/sugarcraft mould. Flock wallpaper can be obtained from most dolls' house suppliers. The ceiling is made by painting and gilding a piece of full-sized embossed paper. At the back is a full dolls'-house-size cabinet house obtained from Andrew Grainger's shop and on top of it is a tiny clock from Past and Present. The carpet is made by cutting up a table mat.

In the kitchen are a resin chef and a cook. The mantelpiece is from The Cat's Whiskers and has been painted to look like wood using a product called Weathered Wood, which can now be obtained from most hobby suppliers. The sink is by Peter Clark and backs on to some tiles made from paper by me. The stove is a simple wooden stove bought from a fair, repaired and black-leaded with acrylic paint and at least four coats of varnish. The dresser and its contents came from The Enchanted Window. The other dresser was made by me and contains a Chrysnbon kitchen set painted to look like spatter ware. This is a very early effort and does not bear close scrutiny except to encourage you to do better!

The room above the kitchen is a housekeeper's room. The two tapestries are from Hilda Burden and most of the other furnishings came from Halcyon. The sofa is a re-upholstered Taiwan sofa. To do this, remove the existing covers very carefully from your chosen suite. Cut new covers from the desired material, allowing a tiny turning – cotton-based or silk materials are easier to use. If your material is slippery, then back it with iron-on Vylene. The lady with the tray is a standard dolls' house resin figure, as is the Pekinese. The chocolate-coloured dog came from Peter Clark.

*Cabinet house kitchen.*

*Cabinet house housekeeper's room.*

*Cabinet house bedroom with lady in hip bath.*

The top bedroom is occupied by a lady taking a bath made by Bustles and Beaus. The bath is on a carpet made from a kit by Hilda Burden. All the lady's clothes, including bloomers, camisole, stockings and the blue dress hanging up on the cupboard, were made by me from cold porcelain. Cold porcelain is a very good way of making items to be left lying around to add a lived-in quality. I sometimes use Milliput to achieve things like hair brushes and clothes brushes because this can be used to join a cameo to a piece of fur fabric if you wish to make a dressing table set of brushes.

Only two of the drawers are occupied by projects. The middle drawer is a large garden with herbaceous borders on either side. Two pieces of railway grass have been laid down and the walls of the drawer have been lined with brick paper. Additional bricks, pillars and sundial were purchased at a fair. The figures are all cake toppers purchased from Basique. The herbaceous border is fixed into dried flower oasis. The greenery is standard greenery from a railway shop plus statice and yarrow, both of which dry well. Small silk flowers from a florist have been cut up and I have made my own sunflowers and other favourites like columbines, violets, cherry blossom and yellow daisies from Cel Craft cutters and cold porcelain. Most of my flowers are attached to the wire used by sugar flower makers, which is the finest wire obtainable. This, too, can be obtained by mail order. The tree is slightly more complicated: I made the trunk by twisting wire together and then covering it with tissue paper to increase the girth; this was then painted with glue, covered with brown-tinted cold porcelain and then textured.

The other garden, which includes a water feature bought at a fair, has a comfortable garden seat from The Dolls House Emporium, a cross little dog statue from Hove and the usual combination of flowers, save that I have included ivy and also my favourable white clematis, which is made with a five-leaf blossom cutter. Each of the petals has to be shaped with a ball tool on a Cel Pad to achieve the right look. You will need to stick leaves and flowers to a spray of wire before sticking it into the border, which is made from oasis.

You can, of course, purchase a new cabinet house, but if you want an old, or at least an old-looking house (the real thing costs a fortune), you will need to keep an eye on car boot sales and junk shops for a suitable cupboard. Old cupboards, particularly those that are moderately priced, need to be checked for woodworm and structural damage. Do not, under any circumstances, import an item with woodworm into your house without treating it first. Take advice from your local ironmonger as to suitable products. I clean old cupboards either with proprietary picture restoring fluid, which can be obtained from an art shop, or with

*Cabinet house garden details.*

a mixture of methylated spirits, button polish and turpentine substitute in equal parts; try a small inconspicuous area first. You will need to 'kill' the cleaning fluid with water. This is not a job to be done indoors and you should follow the instructions on health and safety given on the bottle or tin. The same products can be used to clean old dolls' houses, although I should stress that anything that may be old and valuable should be checked out with an expert before you start, in case your cleaning efforts diminish its value.

# GEORGIAN PERIOD

Purely in the interest of research, I expect many of you will have watched *Tom Jones* on the television. I enjoyed the adventures of Sophia and Tom, particularly in their best clothes of course, and I also liked Brian Blessed's portrayal of Squire Western. Television dramas are a painless and even enjoyable way of seeing how particular historical periods fit together visually. The heyday of the Georgian period was from 1730–95,

*Georgian house front.*

during which period here were three Georges: George I (1714–27), George II (1727–60) and George III (1760–1820). George III's son, the Prince of Wales, due to his father's recurring illness, ruled from 1811–20 as Prince Regent and then for a further ten years as King: the Regency style is also popular with miniaturists.

School textbooks tend to refer to the Georgian period as the 'Age of Enlightenment' because of the great flowering of cultural and scientific achievement. Joshua Reynolds, Thomas Gainsborough and William Hogarth all provide vivid portraits of this period, and the composers Bach, Handel and Mozart flourished. If you were wealthy, your house could have been designed by Robert Adam and furnished by the likes of Thomas Chippendale.

The beginnings of the Industrial Revolution meant that for the wealthy there was a considerable increase in wealth. The upper middle classes lived in what seems to have been a golden age, but life for the poor and for the common soldier – and this was a period which was not spared military activity – must have been much bleaker. This period saw the beginning of the modern United States of America, the French Revolution, the East India Company's struggle for supremacy in India and the Seven Years' War. It also saw, of particular interest to me, the beginnings of the City of London as a financial centre. In 1773 the Stock Exchange was founded.

Georgian architecture is sometimes seen as a mishmash of classical features such as pediments, columns and pilasters. These can be seen in mock Georgian terraced houses constructed by modern architects, but are not really the essence of Georgian architecture. Robert Morris, the first published English Palladian theorist, said 'proportion is the first principle and proper appropriation of the parts constituting symmetry and harmony'. Like others of his school, he hoped that the mathematical

ideals of architecture based on Palladio and ultimately Plato would enable designers to mirror the 'ideal beauty' of nature itself. For me, the charm of Georgian architecture is that it is quintessentially British. From the smallest country house to stately homes, it is pleasing to the eye. There is an endless supply of Georgian houses to draw and I spent many lunch hours when working in the City of London drawing houses in Bedford Row, Lincoln's Inn and Albany Street. I have also visited a number of stately homes, as a member of the National Trust.

A number of factors worked together to prompt my Georgian projects. I purchased a Georgian-style country house from Bryan Frost. I have been able to buy two useful books: *The Georgian Group Book of the Georgian House* by Steven Parisian was intended for the lucky owners of real Georgian houses, but the pictures and details apply just as much to half scale; and *Georgian House Style* by Ingrid Cranfield is particularly useful for details of furniture and vital bits of information about kitchens and sanitation. The National Trust also publish a little book entitled *Household Management* which is full of useful pictures of rooms which visitors did not generally see, such as kitchens, lavatories, nurseries and so on. This book covers all periods, not just Georgian.

Then, of course, there were the Georgian gardens such as those designed by Lancelot Brown, later nicknamed 'Capability Brown' from his habit of referring to the 'capabilities' of sites on which he was consulted for his work. Thomas Chippendale designed some delightful garden furniture; no fashionable garden was complete without its classical temple or reinterpreted Gothic gazebo.

As luck would have it, my plans were given a final boost as I was able to buy a pile of old Sotheby's catalogues at a jumble sale which proved to be full of splendid carpets and wall hangings, with lots of photographs of pictures and china.

An excellent way of seeing the evolution of style in the British house is to visit the miniature house collection at Hever Castle in Kent.

In the Georgian House it can be seen that increasing importance is given to private family life. Georgian households had two-room suites, which were called lodgings, for each member of the family. In Palladian-style houses, the most important reception rooms were not on the ground floor, but on the 'piano nobile', or first floor. Unfortunately, achieving mathematically perfect gracious architectural proportions does not make for comfort and convenience, particularly in the matter of kitchen facilities, hot dinners and accommodation for servants. Kitchens and servants' accommodation were often housed in another wing away from the main block of the house. Some houses had covered passageways. Grand reception rooms were used for dancing, taking tea or coffee and playing cards or gambling with dice.

Tea drinking began in the 1660s and became the last word in fashion among the nobility. Tea was expensive and was made in the saloon or in the drawing room by the lady of the house herself, not by a servant. *The Antiques Road Show* quite frequently has typical tea caddies and also the silver sets including a silver kettle which worked over a spirit lamp. The growing vogue for tea and for coffee- and chocolate-drinking helped the Wedgwood Potteries founded by Josiah Wedgwood to flourish.

Robert Adam, who was one of the most famous interior designers of the mid-Georgian period, believed that dining rooms, in particular, required special design and care because of the conversation which took place during and after dinner. After the ladies withdrew, the gentlemen would discuss business, politics and, no doubt, religion. Pattern books of the time show wine coolers, sideboards, cutlery containers, plate racks, lamps for warming, no doubt,

very cold food and every sort of period gadget. To save missing fascinating conversation, some Georgian sideboards were even fitted with the means for gentlemen to relieve themselves without having to leave the room. Both Greek or Roman and Egyptian decorations were fashionable, as well as that style of particularly Georgian decoration which was exported across to the United States and is now seen so beautifully executed in the Thorne Rooms.

I shall first deal with the external decoration of the house.

The exterior of the Manor was painted by applying a coat of ochre paint with a silk sponge. This gives the effect of stucco without being as overwhelming as dolls' house stucco or, worse still, polyfilla can be in small scale. I then sponged this with other shades of brown, rust and grey to give the effect of old stonework. The downstairs brick floors are made from brick paper. Upstairs, the carpets are from auction catalogues. Panelling is made by staining the walls with wood stain and then staining half scale beading to match. The plasterwork and fireplaces are home-made as before.

One of the most exciting aspects of modelling, for me, is to discover a whole new area of parts and ideas, particularly for the smaller scales (half and quarter). Being married to a keen railway modeller, I go to a number of railway shows as well as dolls' house shows. My find of the month, so to speak, was the Langley Masterbuild Building Kits Handbook. This is intended for one of the commonest railway scales, OO, which equates to ⅛in scale. It also contains a number of parts which are extremely useful for half and quarter scale modelling when used other than for their designated purpose.

This brings me back to the problems of my Georgian house and, in particular, to achieving suitably scaled architectural mouldings and fireplaces. My problems were to some extent self-induced. I wanted grand Georgian-style fireplaces. These

*Georgian house detail.*

exist in ½ scale in profusion, while the supply is not so varied and quite expensive in half scale and non-existent in quarter scale; until, that is, I got to the Langley stall. Their cast window frames, particularly combined with cornice board and party-wall corbels, make excellent components for a variety of fireplaces, bookcases and twiddly bits. Because these are made of white metal, they are easy to cut with a modelling saw and, once undercoated, can be painted with acrylic or oil paint.

For parts of my fireplaces, I used arches intended for front/French doors, Victorian, Georgian and fluted pilasters, and I also used some corbels as brackets. You get twelve of these in a packet and they make excellent shelf brackets as well. To add variety, I have used some of my own home-made architectural mouldings.

The method of basic assembly for a drawing room or bedroom fireplace is as follows. Cut a piece of polyboard to the right size for your chimney breast – you may wish to cut out a section as shown in the photo for a grate. Using tacky glue, stick your mouldings to the polyboard. I used a small piece of cardboard or plasticard from my scrap box to make a shelf for the mantlepiece. The actual fire back is created from embossed wall paper. Phoenix now make small castings of the interior of fire surrounds and grates. If you wish to have a mirror above the fireplace, you will find that the smaller ½ scale frames or a suitably shaped jewellery finding can be used. Stick it in the desired position with tacky glue. I used the lids of Chinese takeaway boxes as mirror glass; do not add these until after painting.

The next step is to spray the whole assembly with car spray undercoat – I used red oxide. My top coat is a mixture of gold metallic and metallic black and red, highlighted with touches of gold marker. The fire backs were sprayed separately with matt black. If you would like to have fire irons, these can be made up out of cocktail sticks and jewellery findings or, alternatively, Phoenix now sell a smaller-scale kit which includes a traditional coal scuttle.

In the pink bedroom is a chaise and dressing table which I made up from a d.ann Ruff kit. You will see that I have also dressed the four-poster bed by Denise Woods with pleated lace. Rose makers – the things that you twiddle silk ribbon on hoping to get silk roses – are widely available. These are terrific for $\frac{1}{2}$ scale but much too large and overwhelming in smaller scales. I made mine by cutting out a section of very fine lace and dying it with appropriately coloured fabric paints. I will be honest and admit that the first few didn't work too well, but it's a useful skill once one has got the knack of it. In many of the rooms are some lovely bone china with applied flowers from Ottervale China in Devon. Aren't the flowers incredibly dainty?

In some ways the producers of costume dramas have an easier life than miniaturists. It is unlikely that plumbing details or how people washed their clothes and, indeed, themselves will form an important part of a television plot. This is quite different from real life, where major family rows can start over whose turn it is to use or clean the bathroom. Even in half scale, it's quite easy to obtain suitable miniature bathroom fittings.

A survey among school children of my acquaintance revealed that they all have a pretty good idea that the Romans were very keen on washing and, indeed, on central heating. A recent *Time Team* television programme showed a sophisticated plumbing system complete with a garderobe which emptied directly down a shaft straight into a moat or ditch. In the interests of authenticity, I had to find out how Tom and Sophie managed and, indeed, how the ladies and gentlemen who attend the assembly in my other Regency house got ready for their parties or, indeed, managed from day to day. As a child visiting France on holiday I

remember being tremendously impressed by the glorious marble temples full of Ormolu gilding and bronze in Versailles and also by the close stool often luxuriously covered in velvet or silk. These were very throne-like though they must have been difficult to keep clean, and also expensive.

In England, Chatsworth is recorded as having a bathing room with blue and white marble walls and multi-coloured marble decorations, stone floor and a blue-veined marble bath with steps down. This even had 'private glass'. Now, as anyone who has ever stood on a marble floor will tell you, marble is expensive and also extremely cold. Apart from stately homes, the majority of people would have taken baths relatively rarely in their bedrooms and the baths would have been made of various metals, wood or pottery. For the most part, people would have kept clean by washing using a basin and jug. You will see that I have obtained a cast metal set from JoJay Crafts and painted it to match a little pink and white washstand chosen for Sophie's bedroom.

It is now possible to obtain facsimile reproductions of the books produced by famous cabinet makers of the period. Thomas Sheraton first published the *The Cabinet Maker and Upholstery Drawing Book* in 1791. There are elegant designs for corner basin stands, for wash hand stands and for pot cupboards. I quote, but with modern spelling:

These are used in genteel bedrooms and are sometimes finished in satinwood and in a style a little elevated above their use. The two drawers below the cupboard are real. The partitions may be cross banded with a string around the corners of the drawer. Their feet are turned but sometimes they are made square. Sometimes there are folding doors to the cupboard parts and sometimes a curtain of green silk fixed on a brass wire at the top and bottom but in this design a Tambour door is used as preferable. The upper cupboard contains shelves and is intended to keep medicines to be taken in the night or hold other

*Georgian house detail.*

little articles which servants are not permitted to overlook!

George Hepplewhite, in the third edition of *The Cabinet Maker and Upholsterers Guide* of 1794, shows elaborate designs for shaving tables, bidet tables, night tables and basin stands. There is also a range of pot cupboards. As well as these items, of course, your well brought-up girl would have had a dressing table complete with the current range of perfumes and pomades.

It needs to be remembered that although a bath in front of the fire is still a luxury, this was then the prerogative of a wealthy family. All water, hot and cold, clean and dirty and the contents of chamber pots had to be carried up and down stairs. It is likely that in an age where labour was cheap, plumbing facilities and bathrooms did not seem to be particularly desirable. Water would be heated in enormous coppers every morning by the kitchen servants.

The earliest commercial patent holder for a water closet was one Joseph Bramah in 1778. The patent drawings show a water closet worked by valves and there is some evidence to suggest that these were successful, at least in the cities among the wealthy. It would have been unlikely in a country house of the rather modest sort that I am dealing with to have such an arrangement. Suitable chamber pots, jugs and basins can be obtained from JoJay Crafts.

It is sometimes possible to obtain a suitable piece of Chinese resin furniture with a mirror, lamp, hair brushes and the like on it. Suitably sized pomade boxes and perfume bottles can be made from very small glass beads using Fimo rolled into tiny balls or other shapes as stoppers. I find that small jewellery findings and, indeed, small $\frac{1}{2}$ scale frames make satisfactory mirrors for dressing tables.

The panelling throughout the house has been made from embossed wallpaper which I have either painted to resemble paintwork and plaster or dyed with wood stain and shoe dye if I wanted an oak-panelled effect. Wallpaper has been cut from writing paper or the inside of envelopes; I have to admit that I mostly ignored the envelopes which accompany my everyday mail at work until an article by Carol Newman prompted me to look at these from the point of view of ¼₄ scale. There are a huge range of designs which are suitable for wallpaper and tiles. Junk mail watching can quickly accumulate a satisfactory range.

In the kitchen I used a resin set from Verlinden purchased from the Harrow Model Shop but obtainable from most suppliers of ⅓₂ scale soldiers. This included an iron range, a dresser and a dry sink. Resin is a challenge to the novice modeller, as the pieces have to be carefully trimmed with a sharp knife and then cleaned of grease. I use warm water with a little soap and vinegar before undercoating with spray-on car paint. It goes without saying that the majority of kitchen fittings in full-size stately homes from the Georgian and Regency period have been replaced by more modern fittings. Household management books of the period tend to be idiosyncratic and to concentrate on family recipes for food and medicines. It is likely, however, that floors would have been stone, walls would have been painted with white- or blue-tinted limewash. Dressers and fitted units would have been scrubbed wood, or perhaps painted, though there was the potential for lead poisoning. My storage jars are part of the Verlinden set or from Phoenix. The larger terracotta items come from the Dolls' House Potter. Both the kitchen table and the dining room table and chairs are Phoenix models. The dry sink in the kitchen has been given the appearance of being full of water by the use of varnish poured on top of dark paint. The cleaning utensils and buckets are from a Phoenix set.

With so many small items to paint for a half scale house kitchen, this is perhaps a good place to remind everybody of the old model soldiers painting trick. Fix your very small items to a piece of balsa wood before you paint them, using double-sided tape or Blu-Tack. It is much easier to spray large numbers of items with car paint at once, as well as being more economical, and it is easier to handle small items stuck-down than to try to hold each individual item to paint it. Double-sided tape and Blu-Tack are less likely to leave a greasy finish which will resist paint.

I decided to make the large room at the top of Sophie and Tom's house into a nursery and school room. In pride of place is a beautiful little jewelled globe of the world from The Treasury in Pinner. The smallest size of wooden dolls were bought at the fair at Hove. There is a little cradle from veneer and some dolls furniture from quarter scale plastic items. There is a hobby horse from Frontshop Miniatures and a wooden rocking horse from Hove. The toy soldiers have been made from railway figures.

Morley Improving Board Games have existed since the eighteenth and early nineteenth centuries. Several members of the Bowles family worked in London as print and map sellers; their *Journey through Europe or the Play of Geography* was printed for Carrington Bowles in 1759, consisting of a map of Europe mounted on canvas and hand coloured. I have used a very tiny map for this.

Education for girls still encompassed a great deal of needlework in the Georgian era. There are two needlework baskets and a pile of mending. You could also include bricks, bats, balls and a hoop.

# STOCKBROKER TUDOR

One of my clients kindly introduced me to this house. He was right. It did 'scrub up lovely' and I have included it in this book as a reminder of the basic techniques of dolls' house restoration and cleaning. Cleaning

*Stockbroker Tudor exterior* (top) *and interior* (bottom).

*Stockbroker Tudor bedroom.*

*Stockbroker Tudor billiards room.*

*Stockbroker Tudor kitchen.*

*Stockbroker Tudor living room.*

beautiful houses bought in antique shops or at auction houses such as Sothebys is a job for experts: as a general rule, always seek advice if your house in any way resembles those shown in any of the classic texts by Constance Eileen King or Vivian Green. This stockbroker Tudor, however, does not fall into that class: it had possibilities once I got it home but it was very, very dirty.

I took the top layer of dirt off using a soft non-woven cloth and then repeated the process with the addition of warm water with baby shampoo. Some of the outside had patches of decaying varnish. For these

I used a proprietary picture cleaner applied with cotton buds. Always test an unobtrusive area first if using one of these products: clean your test area, neutralize the product in accordance with the manufacturer's instructions and then leave the test area to settle down for at least two days.

The inside of my house had been decorated with full-scale fifties-style wallpaper and some full-sized but attractively faded carpet samples. Wallpaper and, indeed all paper products, need to be left well alone in old houses. I use a tiny vacuum cleaner intended for computer keyboards and other high-tech equipment; this will take off much of the dust. Also useful are a kind of sticky glove which picks up dust, fluff, animal hair and the accumulation of lint and other nasties that second-hand dolls' houses tend to have.

If you have missing wallpaper it is often possible to take a colour photocopy of an intact piece and use this to replace the missing bit. You can use diluted cold tea and coffee to age the paper. The woodwork inside the house, principally on the stairs, was cleaned with paint restorer. I covered the wallpaper, carpet and anything else that looked vulnerable with polythene held down with masking tape. I suppose this is the miniaturists' equivalent of dust sheets!

Once clean, the only structural repairs needed were repairs to a crack in the roof which I fixed with modern wood glue. Since this crack was unpleasant to look at, I covered the whole of the roof with slate paper which somebody had already used round the front door, and also used paper paving slabs round the base board which was a mixture of plain wood and some Fablon which had obviously been added later and did nothing for the house.

As all good miniaturists know, no project is ever really complete. This house, as you will see, is waiting for some suitable curtains. I've tried various sources and have now reached the stage of waiting to see what turns up. Old fabrics are somehow better in old houses and these are likely to be found in somebody's attic or rag box, a jumble sale, a car boot sale or even a charity shop.

The house has four rooms, a hall and a spacious landing. The bedroom photographed to look like night time is furnished with Taiwan furniture. I used a Chrysnbon dressing table set and washstand and potty set. The various brand items such as cold cream, cough medicine, Milk of Magnesia, 4711 Eau de Cologne and so on were purchased, though I have toned down the labels with a little cold tea.

My lady in the bath, who is the old gentleman asleep in the double bed's fantasy, came from Freda Dorgan; the bath was a birthday present. The games room has a little upright piano.

The snooker table came from the Dolls House Emporium and the musical instruments are Christmas decorations. These tend to tarnish after a while: the trick is to varnish them with spray varnish as soon as you have bought them so that the shine doesn't fade. My cats and dogs are from Woolworths and have been toned down or repainted with acrylic paints.

The furniture in the kitchen was assembled from a kit from Panduro Hobby. Again, I tried to achieve authentic products in the kitchen. The stove came from a car boot sale and has Aga-type lids made with buttons. The demijohn for home wine-making was made by Leo Pulley. The two cats on a cushion are by Peter Clark.

The sitting room is a jumble of my disjointed memories of my mother's wartime escapades. You can see a wartime ration book and identity card on the floor with a biscuit tin full of old photographs. Old-fashioned games are on the 'whatnot', which is a very distressed Chrysnbon kit as is the glass-fronted china cabinet. My 1940-style lady with the curlers came from Dolly Clobber. The ARP cat on the hat was a birthday present. I was able to obtain

135

various magazines, little photographs and wartime documents and labels from The Cat's Whiskers. Carol Mann made the beautiful mauve and blue bowl. I really liked the mauve crushed velvet suite, which was from Hilda Burden.

The garden on the front of this house isn't my painting. It was there under all the muck once I had cleared up.

# THE ALCHEMIST'S HOUSE

This is another junk shop find. The previous owner hadn't even bothered to decorate the inside.

The wizard's workroom on the top floor has a ceiling made from embossed paper which has been stained with wood stain and then gilded and painted. The work unit of shelves and drawers was created by cutting down a Dolls House Emporium kit for an old-fashioned chemist's storage unit with lots of little drawers. I made the drawer labels myself by writing suitable ingredients from a book on alchemy and *Culpepper's Herbal*. Beads have been used for little brass handles and similar labels have been done for the storage jars, which I made myself from clay.

The Tudor furniture throughout this house came from Renee Stubbs and Tudor Time, except for the court buffet and the four-poster bed, which were a birthday present. Many of the small wooden items such as bowls, buckets and 'whatnot', are part of a child's kitchen set which I bought in Southall. Originally in whitewood, this was made to look old and medieval by using wood stain and liming wax.

This house also houses some of my collection of miniature pottery. Many of these pieces are made by proper potters, i.e. friends at evening classes, and others are art school's test pieces. The jardiniere is

from Sadie Jocelyn, Carol Mann made the bowls in the kitchen and the pieces on the dresser came from Clive Brooker.

I made the slip-cast saucepans, hot water jug and crockery in the sink myself using a Duncan mould. These were slip cast, fired and then painted with acrylic paints. On the floor of the kitchen are two little rats made by Rosie Duck. The candle stand came from In Some Small Way and the dresser and kitchen table were originally whitewood from Apollo Miniatures. Smoke and other damage has been applied to these using acrylic paint and coloured wax. The stove is quite frankly a cheat and would not bear any close scrutiny. It is a cardboard box with a bead and a drinking straw to which have been added some pieces of plastic scrap and balsa wood. The whole has been sprayed matt black, and two buttons have been used to create the lids.

Flooring in this house came from a number of sources. The bedroom and kitchen have rush matting made from embroidery fabric dyed with cold tea. The main downstairs room has a carpet made from a table mat. The magician's flooring is made from tiles cut from Butterfly sticky paper which has then been varnished over to give the effect of glazed tiles. I used children's stickers from Woolworths in the bedroom to create the mural.

The hangings on the bed I made myself using simple cross stitch and blackwork patterns with one strand of black cotton. These have been embellished with gold and scarlet embroidery floss. The menagerie on top of the four-poster bed was created using hobby ceramic moulds.

Some years ago Duncan, a major hobby ceramic retailer, produced a fantasy range and these little creatures, two ravens, an owl and a small dragon, are part of that range. They were slip cast, fired in my kiln and then painted.

(Top) *Alchemist's shop exterior.*
(Above) *Alchemist's kitchen.*
(Right) *Alchemist's bedroom.*

(Top) *Alchemist's workroom.*                    *Alchemist's living room.*

# HALF SCALE HOTEL

This hotel owes a great deal to Gary at Dolls' House Direct. He supplied the wooden carcass and also a number of boxes of very competitively priced Taiwan resin room sets.

When I was much younger, I had a number of temporary jobs. One of these was in a small family hotel in the Loire valley in France. The decoration and the characters who either stay or work in this hotel are based on my experiences as a temporary hotel chambermaid/waitress.

At the time when I was working in France, hotel bedrooms had by law to have certain essential furnishing. This included somewhere to hang one's clothes, a mirror, a writing table, a chair and a copy of the fire drill, an average menu and the times and prices of meals. The quality of furniture was not specified, and in many hotels furniture which was past its best and no longer appropriate to the restaurant was scrubbed down, repainted and used in the bedrooms. Rather grander bedrooms might have recovered armchairs and sofas. Somewhere to hang clothes varied from a row of hooks to a real wardrobe. French provincial hotels at that time went for something that didn't show the dirt and wore well. In practice, this meant florid flower patterns or paisley.

On the top floor, the yellow bedroom is furnished with a suite made from cold porcelain and canvas. I made a simple frame from moulding canvas and decorated this with some rather tatty gold lampshade braid. The pink room with the little girl in it is furnished with a flat-pack kit which has been deliberately aged with wood stain and liming wax. The original coat of rose pink paint looked much too new and shiny. The blue

*Half scale hotel exterior.*

*Half scale hotel details.*

bedroom has been furnished with a white-wood bedroom set from Apollo Miniatures. I painted this cobalt blue and then applied liming wax with steel wire wool.

On the next floor down are two rather grander suites. The green suite is furnished with a flat-pack bedroom suite which has been decorated with gold marker pen and distressed a little with liming wax and steel wool. The dressing table, chairs, stool and desk have been topped with very fine green leather which has been embossed with a gold gel pen. The rug is

from a d.ann Ruff kit which comes pre-printed. You can then colour the pattern in with a collection of ordinary felt-tip pens. The blue bedroom suite is made from moulding canvas and cold porcelain with matching cushions, seats and drapes.

These larger rooms have bathrooms. One suite was purchased from a shop, the other is made from a flat-pack kit, lined with cold porcelain. The flowers and pot plants were also made from cold porcelain, as are the ceiling roses and the piles of clothes which are waiting to be put away. I hit on cold

(Above) *Half scale hotel bedroom.*

porcelain for this purpose because fabrics become very difficult to handle in smaller scales. Reproducing modern carpet and floor boarding, particularly since I intended to treat it so it looked scruffy, proved difficult until I had a lucky find with Fablon. The green carpet is sticky-back plastic, as are the blond floorboards.

There is no need to worry that the equipment for a minuscule pub or bar might be difficult to find; all the necessary impedimenta like barrels, tills, bottles and so on can be bought from the suppliers listed at the end of this book in all the commonly used scales. Since no self-respecting railway modeller appears to wish to have a layout without a pub, this is not a problem. My bar is supplied with a mixture of items from mail order suppliers and Garden Railway Supplies. The sofas and chairs in the bar and the tea lounge, together with most of the more ornate fittings, are from a resin room box set.

*Half scale hotel detail.*

The reception area has a nice little desk and an elaborate Victorian whatnot from Bespaq. A commercial traveller was made by Freda Dorgan. There is another kit rug at the entrance.

The restaurant is kitted out from an assortment of resin kits. Since some of the place settings were either rather curious or deficient in the right number of plates for the number of chairs, I have added the odd extra cup and saucer or plate from Milliput.

(Above) *Half scale hotel details.*

(Facing page)
*Half scale hotel sitting room* (top).
*Half scale hotel restaurant* (middle).
*Half scale hotel reception area* (bottom).

*Half scale hotel kitchen.*

The kitchen downstairs has been covered with fabric which looks like oilcloth and painted blue, a popular colour for kitchens from the turn of the century onwards because blue was believed to keep flies away! Most of the furnishings are souped-up resin including the stove. Pots, pans, kettles and so on are from Phoenix, painted to look like copper or cast iron. After all, a French chef has to have proper *batterie de cuisine*. An apple flan is being made at one of the kitchen tables; two of the tables are whitewood stained with oak stain and then rubbed down to distress them, and the third is from a flat-pack kit. A few pots and kettle stains have been added using a half scale pan and some appropriately coloured paint.

Chef and his helpers, like the rest of the hotel staff, are made by me from cold porcelain. The chef is reviewing his work and working himself up to lecturing a couple of apprentices about the quality of an omelette which he deems unfit for human consumption. You can understand why the apprentices are hiding in the cellars.

The laundry room contains a collection of old cane chairs made deliberately badly this time from canvas. The sewing machine was a thimble, and the ironing board and two deep freezers are fridge magnets. The washer/dryer is a resin castings and requires careful trimming and painting. For electrical appliances I find that car spray paint gives the best finish.

The exterior of the hotel has been finished in red stucco which has been antiqued with wood stain, and the roof is painted to look like fish-scale tiles. The outdoor café is a common feature of small French hotels even to this day. The seats and parasols come from a kit intended for a garden railway and have been toned down with paint. The outside customers enjoying their cassis, *vin rouge* or even Pernod are also plastic railway figures. This house appears to have built-in cat attraction and at least plastic figures are not easily broken. Hotels and cafés present all sorts of interesting possibilities for miniaturists as do pubs. Not only can you arrange for all sorts of goings-on in the public rooms and, indeed, in the bedrooms but the exterior can have added interest in the form of period vehicles or even a hunt or a vintage car rally.

# Out in the Fresh Air

## AT THE SEASIDE

My seaside scene with its various buildings, playground and even the tiny little bit of sea and the odd rock pool, doesn't normally occupy as much space. The bits and pieces live in our bathroom on a specially cleared shelf. I am sure I caught the seaside bug as a result of seeing the many beautiful beach scenes which have been undertaken as club projects and shown at venues like Alexandra Palace. I salute the members of these clubs: their beautiful workmanship and restrained taste are a model to us all.

My beach scene is the place where I put people who look like real people at their worst, not their best. This is a place for naughty old ladies and even naughtier old men. Exhausted, rather plain parents try to forget that their children are bound to be up to something naughty and probably are at this very moment developing the latest in a long line of undiagnosable spotty allergies.

No wholesome, organic, additive-free food is sold on this beach. The fish stall sells

*Seaside scene.*

*Seaside scene detail.*

Window and I felt I already knew her: she quite obviously came to the seaside to get away from her family and has no intention of swimming. Most of her time is spent knitting and gossiping, sleeping and drinking home-made cocktails mostly made with gin. Their eldest granddaughter, now a teenager, has been bribed to keep an eye on the little ones at the playground. Eventually I must make her a Walkman to alleviate her misery.

Also in the playground are another set of holidaying grandparents. These are very simple wire and bead dolls, and they came as a family set with the children who are on the seesaw. Grandfather is absorbed in his ice-cream. To complete the scene, there are two battered rowing boats purchased from a gift shop. The two dogs are repainted plastic.

burgers, sausages, roe and, of course, fish and real chips fried in lard, served with a side order of gherkins, pickled eggs or pick-led onions, and the kind of sauce that would strip paint. Miniaturists' licence means that these items are still sold wrapped in news-paper. The chip shop owner's complexion is a tribute to the long hours that he puts in. His lady wife runs the tea, cakes and ices stall. Granny is consuming some of the cakes. Tea is stewed with lots of sugar. There are, of course, bottles of various fruit-flavoured drinks which have never been anywhere near the fruits they are named after. Also available are seaside rock, refreshers, lollipops and other ways of attacking juvenile teeth.

There are three levels to this beach scene. Level one is an esplanade with a road which has the two refreshment stalls and a play-ground. Level two is a bit of cliff manufac-tured from a cardboard box. A slightly flatter bit of cliff has Granny's private beach hut. This lady came from The Enchanted

*Sweet stall.*

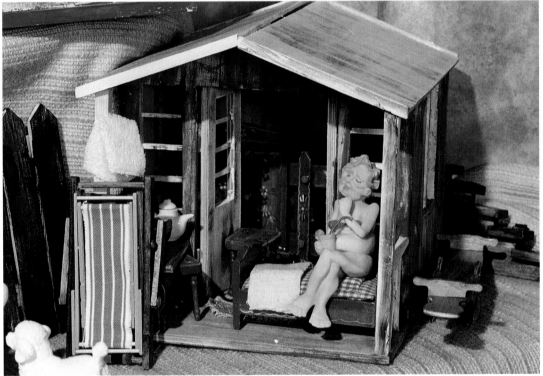

(Top) *Tea stall detail.*                    *Beach hut detail.*

*Beach detail.*

The fish and chip kiosk was purchased at an R and J fair and was made by Pixie Rustics. It is owned by a little rag doll from a well-known chain store who cooks on a plastic stove from a car boot sale. His equipment is white-metal castings painted appropriately with food made from resin or Fimo. His lady wife, a rag doll from the same source, keeps a beautifully fitted transport café from Dolls' House Direct which has a perfect little water boiler and sink, which were pre-fitted. I regret to say that I have knocked the kiosk around a bit to fit it in with the general air of seaside wear and tear.

Sweets in jars and lollipops were made by me. Branded sweets were obtained from Valerie Claire Miniatures. The grannies' beach hut is also from Dolls' House Direct.

Both it and its furniture have been heavily distressed by the use of patina paints, wire wool and liming wax.

A seaside scene should take account of the corrosive effects of salt and seawater. Paint crazes and peels, and all colours fade. Wood becomes bleached out. These effects can be achieved by using crackle glaze, liming wax and wood finishes. The deckchairs on the beach have been aged with a mixture of wood stains and the material has been frayed and dyed with diluted cold tea. White splotches where the pre-assembled chairs had glue and would not take the stain have been disguised with Scuffcoat, a proprietary shoe dye.

The wooden playground furniture, including the bench, is part of a flat-pack kit.

It looked really nice when I first finished it, but achieved its rickety, dusty appearance all by itself on the shelf in my workshop. Sand-castles were made by pushing cold porcelain into a dolls' house doll's sand bucket and a variety of blister packs for pills and cough sweets. These were pre-coloured with sand-coloured paint, a mixture of ochre, sienna and umber, and then sprayed with scatter material and budgie sand. Buckets and spades can be obtained from Valerie Claire.

## FISH TANKS

Some beautiful scenes have been created by other miniaturists in glass fish tanks and traditional glass goldfish bowls.

Much as I would like to use one of these, the cats regard anything large and fragile as a challenge. The fish tank project happened spontaneously while the family were on holiday in Cornwall, and I had taken a kit-house with me. We rent a cottage, which is the only practical holiday solution for two modellers. There is a limit to the number of kits you can pack and the kit-house was already done.

On Tuesday it began to rain and rain and rain. Sticky cakes and bookshops seemed the best option so we went to Penzance for the day. While I waited for my husband to choose his sticky cake, my eye was taken by a delightful little plastic portable room box complete with handle, very reasonably priced. A few seconds later, realization dawned. This was not a room box: it was a kind of small portable aquarium suitable for fish or small rodents. An extremely helpful young lady in the shop explained to me how useful, portable and hygienic these items were and was equally patient when I explained that the plan was to create a

*Neptune fish tank with lid.*

miniature but very dead scene, at least I hope it was all dead, in each of the three sizes. Once I had explained my intentions with drawings on the back of an envelope, she was kind enough to offer a special rate for bulk purchases!

(Above) *Neptune fish tank.*

*Neptune fish tank detail.*

I turned my three matching fish tanks into holiday projects, the first being Neptune's realm under the sea. I painted waves on the outside of the tank with a glass relief paint and filled in the colours with blue and turquoise glass paint, with the odd splash of white for foam. Neptune's scenery was simply created with a bag of aquarium pebbles and artistically piled shells (Cornwall is full of shops selling beautiful shells). Neptune himself sits on a gold carved throne. The two dolphins appear to be made from balsa wood and were bought in a gift shop. My gorgeous tropical fish came from the Early Learning Centre.

Neptune was created from a Cel Craft cake icing mould. I used the general method described on page 101, moulding the head over a cotton ball and the body over an armature composed of a loop of wire for stability filled in with tinfoil. The pleated drifty clothes are achieved by frilling thinly rolled paste on a yellow sponge block called a Cel Pad with a smocking tool and ceramic texturizing tools. Neptune's hair was created by squeezing cold porcelain through a garlic press. His trident is a bit of bamboo skewer suitably painted and, again, decorated with bits of cold porcelain.

The mermaids required several attempts. Eventually, I made a simple tail shape over an armature of crushed tinfoil. The trick is to arrange the tinfoil in the shape you want before you cover it with cold porcelain. Texture is added with a texturizing tool or, in my case, the top of a chipped ball-point pen. If all else fails, use half a drinking straw. Bodies and arms were made over a foil armature. The arms are made with a Cel Craft mould, as are the heads. The hair is made by using a smocking tool over thinly rolled pre-coloured yellow paste which is then separated with a pair of small scissors and curled round a cocktail stick or knitting needle. I discovered that less is more with mermaids' faces: do not add too much detail and resist the urge to use elaborate makeup.

Seaweed is either railway foliage or ribbons of cold porcelain draped to dry in natural shapes over a variety of kitchen utensils, such as wooden spoons and spatulas. Texture has been added with smocking tools and embossing tools, and I pre-coloured the paste with green gouache. The advantage with mermaids is that they don't wear clothes, although I have arranged my mermaids' hair so no offence is given to delicately brought-up readers!

# AT THE BOTTOM OF MY GARDEN

Most dolls' house books include historical projects, which tend to stop sometime in the 1930s or at the end of the Second World War; this project is intended to be right up to date. During the summer I work in a studio in the garden which is basically a glorified – if that is the right word – shed improved over the years with things like shelves and a sink. I am also a keen gardener, so if the studio isn't far enough from unwelcome distractions, there is always the greenhouse, which is right out of reach of the television, the telephone and the fax.

This little complex was a wooden shell made specially for me by Tom's Miniatures. It includes a shed which is a great deal tidier and better fitted than the full-size original, a nesting box, a bird table, a seat – not for me, but for my cats – a rabbit hutch for the various beasties who live with us temporarily as lodgers from a local vet, and a water butt. The water butt is a Peter Clark special, complete with blue tit and puddle underneath. There is a wooden fence round the property which is in much better order than the original. The base and path have been covered with railway gravel.

The whole of the project was stained with walnut stain. I then realized that, even if the originals were this colour, the finished

151

(Above) *My garden.*

*My garden detail.*

project would photograph badly, so I have lightened some areas with liming wax to improve the final photograph.

Just like everybody else's workshop, mine is full of projects which are half-finished or in progress. I keep my bits and pieces in a variety of cardboard and plastic containers, usually the sort which are given away free or are meant to be used as vegetable racks or kitchen storage. The three little houses which are unfinished, stained, not painted, and complete, are plaster of Paris castings from an egg-crafter. The tools which appear in the picture as well are exquisite: they were made by James Hickling of Masterpiece Miniatures. Small figures in various states of unfinished-ness on the shelves have been assembled, or perhaps I mean disassembled, from railway figures. Bricks, window frames, timber, brick paper and components are also from ¼₄ gauge suppliers. My scrapbook, glue pot and scraps were purchased at Hove. The assortment of paint cans, bottles of stain, paper and old rags came from my scrap box.

*My garden, workshop interior.*

*My garden, greenhouse interior.*

Most dolls' house suppliers sell scissors and paints, as well as small jars of glass or plastic which can be painted or filled. The newspaper on the bench has been created by distressing pages from out-of-date legal textbooks. The method for making cold porcelain flowers is described on page 63. I created pansies and other spring flowers for my greenhouse; these have been used with railway foliage and very small dried flowers to create an assortment of pots of flowers. I have to say that in real life these would be nothing like as neat and tidy, as my eldest cat takes a malevolent delight in either digging up or sleeping on any newly-filled pot of bedding plants. The tools in the greenhouse were purchased as white metal blanks, filed and painted. The two Grecian urns, one with white flowers and one with orange, were a birthday present. Similar items can be obtained commercially, or you can make your own using Fimo or cold porcelain. On the bench outside the greenhouse is a cat and beside it is my usual half-drunk cup of coffee.

Of course if this were real life, the scene would also include a telephone extension and my portable phone, not to mention a clock, but I have used poetic licence and excluded these items.

# THE ROMAN GARDEN

This little corner of a Roman garden was inspired by reading a series of Lindsey Davis's books on holiday and by the fountain which I found in a souvenir shop. It actually works with real water and, if allowed to, will even play a tune. I used the polystyrene packaging that the fountain was packed in to make the walls of the garden. These were painted with acrylic paint which was then shaded and sponged, and finally dry-brushed to look like an old grey limestone wall.

The two figures are made from cold porcelain. The young man is wearing a simple tunic with a handkerchief tied round his neck and Roman sandals, which are glued to a completely rigid cold-porcelain figure. The texture is achieved with a smocking tool and by dry-brushing white paint and then a little brown on the pre-coloured tunic paste, once it has been assembled on the figure. Hair is made by texturing and then cutting strands to look like locks of hair once the wig is in place.

The lady on the couch, who is definitely a social class or two up from her gentleman friend, wears a simple shift dress. Her hairstyle is made from a piece of cold porcelain that has been textured with a smocking tool; a further strip was then textured with the same tool and twisted to make a chignon, and a few loose curls have been made from scraps pushed through a sieve.

*Roman garden.*

*Roman garden.*

The tiny earrings are just blobs painted with metallic paint. Again, she wears sandals but, if you look, you will see that these are tied rather more elegantly.

Grape and ivy leaves were made from cold porcelain with Cel Craft cutters. It is essential to colour leaves in a project like this in a variety of colours, and once the leaves have been fixed to the tendrils of wire that form the main stalk, they should also be antiqued and dry-brushed. My bunches of grapes are a cheat: I found some artificial flowers which appeared to be composed of little globules of polystyrene which painted up well and look just like young grapes. There are two potted plants in the garden. One is a lemon tree with leaves and fruit made from cold porcelain and a trunk made by covering a wire with cold porcelain. Pre-colour the paste and try not to make the lemons too large. The daisy-type plant (I had a long argument with a classical scholar as to what sort of roses the Romans would have had and eventually gave up) is made with a Cel Craft cutter. I have treated the pot with a verdigris finish.

Cushions are made from cold porcelain textured with a silk tool and painted with pearlized paint. The Alsatian dog came from the Dolls House Emporium. The couch was a work kit from Brooklea Crafts which I painted blue and then dry-brushed; the carving is from a Cel Craft cake mould. A piece of marbled flooring is surrounded by a path, again made from cold porcelain, which makes remarkably good cobbles and is cheap to use. You just press a thin sheet into the mould, leave it to dry (you may have to press it to keep it flat) and when it is dry, paint, antique and varnish it.

*Wall house exterior.*
(Above) *Wall house interior.*
(Below) *Wall house roof with dragon.*

# ——18——

# Complexes

## TUDOR VILLAGE ON A SHELF

Tudor period houses with part-timbering and the distinctive black and white appearance associated with Shakespeare's Stratford are popular with miniaturists. For most of us a complete village is impossible in ½ scale. A small hamlet becomes possible in half scale since one can fit eight half scale houses into the space occupied by one ½ scale house. There are at present four buildings in this village: three made by Bryan Frost and sold as plain wood shells, and one by Sue and Alan's Little Treasures, supplied decorated inside and out with a lighting system.

The first house is intended to hang on the wall like a picture – a useful space-saving quality. I have created a rather curious veterinary establishment, intended for wizards who wish to train in the healing art associated with mythical animals. The nature of the business is indicated by the small red dragon, formerly an earring, hanging at the front. (Universal literacy did not arrive until Victorian times: prior to that most commercial premises indicated their wares by pictures or carved signs.)

The house exterior was quite simple. I stained the entire house with Jacobean oak stain and then the bits between the beams were painted with textured paint which was, in turn, dry-brushed with ochre, grey

*Wall house interior.*

*Wall house.*

and a little mossy green. Although Tudor buildings do appear to be white from a distance, as a house ages it becomes dirty and various sorts of vegetation coat the lath and plaster work.

The roof of the house is covered is small slates cut from Peter Clark's slate system. This can be made to look very realistic by antiquing it with a wash of walnut-coloured stain and then dry-brushing a little light grey to highlight the odd slate. Please remember that old roofs tend to have chipped and slipping slates.

The inside of the house is equally simple. I have opted for plain Jacobean oak-panelled rooms and stained the stairs and ladder to the attic and the floorboards in the same way. The furnishings are also relatively simple. The attic is used to accommodate in-patients: three dragon-shaped fridge magnets have been heavily antiqued and one deliberately broken. They now loll around doing as well as can be expected on cushions

stuffed with straw. Small buckets of coal and water as well as the remains of last night's dinner lurk around: the coal is railway coal and the buckets were bought. The dinner is served on a long wooden bowl, one of those small wooden shapes sold by hobby supermarkets. Dinner is made from meat-coloured cold porcelain chopped up into small bits with some small pieces of plastic from the spare bits left after assembling a kit, chopped up to look like bone.

The schoolroom is furnished with an exquisite set of barley-twist chairs and matching table, made to commission by Masters Miniatures. The ornate shelves behind have been made from balsa wood and mouldings made with cold porcelain and a cake icing mould. The whole has then been stained with wood stain. I made the wooden feed bins from small wooden barrels sold by railway suppliers and also by dolls' house suppliers. The smaller jars are made from Phoenix metal castings and an assortment of beads with lids and sometimes bottoms made from cold porcelain. Some of these have illegible handwriting: you could make similar labels by using certain decorative typefaces on a computer or word processor. Three small wizard pupils stand suffering, as do students and apprentices everywhere, while the master wizard attempts to explain how to convert the frog into a prince.

In the consulting rooms downstairs waits a pig who would now like to go back to being a human being, a maiden with a couple of frogs (I think we all know what she wants) and two large and rather oddly coloured salamanders. The consulting room has two chairs made from fretwork. Like those in all consulting rooms, the waiting seats are rather basic and uncomfortable and the reading matter old and tattered. This is made from the pages of a legal textbook cut up and rolled into scrolls after suitable distressing and treatment with tea and walnut stain.

The second house in this village first made its appearance in *Dolls House and Miniature Scene*'s 'Projects Magazine' as a Christmas house. Christmas is being celebrated by a family of gorgeously dressed mice from Perri Miniatures. I liberated a suitably sized Father Christmas tree ornament from a well-known DIY chain and repaired the chips with sculpture paste before repainting.

Bryan Frost's house was sold as an unpainted wooden shell. I stained the woodwork with Jacobean oak stain diluted one-third with methylated spirit. The exterior of the house was coated with thick tacky glue and then a layer of air-hardening clay which was scribed to look like stone. This was painted with walnut acrylic antiquing solution and then randomly dry-brushed with grey ochre and stone acrylics. The

*Wall house.*

*Tudor watermill interior.*

(Below) *Tudor watermill interior.*

wooden quoins have been coated with textured paint, as have the lintels and window sills. The roof is made from narrow corrugated card scribed to look like roof tiles and painted with terracotta and various shades of green and black.

Inside, the house has been painted with a warm peach from a match pot sample of emulsion. It has then been dulled down with very diluted walnut stain and aged by using liming wax. Stairs and ladders to the attic have been stained with pine wood stain. The flat-pack furniture much loved by miniaturists is now available in half scale as well as $\frac{1}{2}$ scale; also used is a set of Taiwan furniture. The bureau in the sitting room, the washing machine and the stove are all fridge magnets. I used an assortment of suitably distressed Taiwan furniture and bits of kit furniture which I had not been terribly successful with, to fill up the attics.

At Christmas time the shop, which is furnished with a Cassidy kit, sells a variety of Christmas specials. The Father Christmas statuettes are collected over the years from fairs and are generally sold as Christmas tree decorations. Christmas fabrics are available from most dolls' house suppliers. The ring toy and the hobby horse and the exquisite tea set came from Frontshop Miniatures. Boxes, carrier bags and other Christmas paraphernalia can now be obtained in $\frac{1}{24}$ scale and I have made a miniature Christmas dinner.

The whatnot in the kitchen with a collection of teapots on it was made by Coombe Crafts. Many of the decorations were cut from a piece of Christmas fabric and stiffened with glue and iron-on Vylene. The wreaths and festoons are made from a single strand of green chenille wool. Carpets are made either by painting a design on thin velvet or by cutting out clippings from a magazine. These can be improved by painting a thin coat of matt varnish on the front and backing them with cotton.

My window blinds were made from a well-washed piece of pillow edging which was slightly tinted with cold tea. The bench was made by Phoenix.

Outside the houses, the grass is railway grass sold by the sheet. My topiary trees came from The Bat's Wing in Alfriston. A small horse was a lucky chain-store purchase. Most chain stores which sell toys also sell plastic animals and, indeed, some useful plastic people. These can be improved by careful painting.

The third house in my complex is a watermill. Again, the structure was made by Bryan Frost. Bricks and slates and the flagstones in the kitchen are made by Peter Clark's building materials. The furniture inside is simple. The attic contains barrels

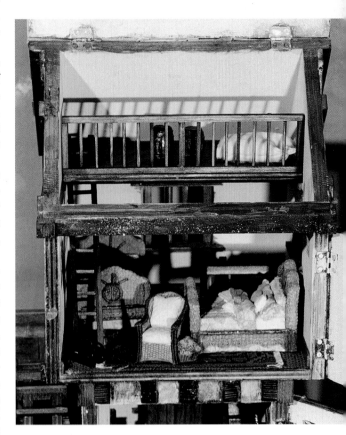

*Tudor watermill interior.*

161

(stained walnut) and sacks from railway suppliers. The bedroom has a charming wicker suite made in resin and sold as a set. The carpet is made from fabric with fringing stuck on. The sampler is computer generated and the angel pictures are from gift tags. The doctor's bag came from Just-in-Case. There is a little fretwork screen purchased at Hove. On the ground floor is a small Phoenix stove and a beautiful settle made by David Lee. The clock is also from Phoenix and the pewter ware is made by Tony Knott.

As a child, I spent some years living in a house which was afflicted by dry rot as well as many other nasty insects and fungal complaints. This gives timber a slightly luminous quality which I have attempted to emulate with moss green paint with a little silver mixed in and very sparingly dry-brushed.

My last house is a pub called the 'Shepherd's Rest'. Again, there is a pictorial sign. On the top floor are two beds made from cold porcelain which has been pre-coloured and then dry-brushed after assembly. The beds are made over a polystyrene base. This is not the stuff sold for ceiling tiles, but a much denser and finer grained version sold for the cake icing market; do not attempt to use it in conjunction with the kind of modelling clay which has to be hardened in the oven.

The middle room has been decorated as a parlour. A tabby cat is investigating under

*Public house interior.*
(Left) *Public house exterior.*

*Public house interior.*

the table made from a Denise Woods' kit. The figures in this room and in the public bar downstairs are made from cold porcelain using a Cel Craft fairy mould.

## HO TERRACE

This is a whole street on a shelf. These projects are built in OO scale, which is close to ⅛ scale. A bout of ⅛ scale modelling was induced by a recent visit to the Pendon Museum. If you have not already been to Pendon then I really recommend a visit: not only are the exteriors of all the houses and other buildings exquisitely modelled and supplied with gardens so authentic that they sell postcards of them in the shop, but many of the models are fully furnished too. There is also a large stock of useful modelling guides and a variety of modellers' accessories, some of which I have used to liven up my street scene.

I love L. S. Lowrie's pictures and the factory buildings and terraced houses are ideal as a backdrop to a Lowrie scene. The factory buildings and the terraced houses are from Cove Models, made from expanded polystyrene. I found that after I had primed them with the coat of car undercoat, they could be easily painted with artists' opaque acrylics with the occasional use of gold and silver fibre-pens for details. It is important with plastic kits to allow the acrylic paint to dry properly between coats and to varnish with matt or satin spray-on varnish for added protection after painting is completed.

The other source of shop models, which have the additional advantage of a front window that can be filled (*see* below), is Langley Models. Their 'V18' set includes three different shop fronts and three Tudor timbered and Georgian upper storeys. Included in the kit are plastic formings for three shops, three upper storeys,

*HO village.*

curtains, brass etchings for all windows, doors and the balcony, cast metal parts for windows, dormer windows, small windows, dormer fittings, Georgian windows, double Georgian windows and a balcony floor and roof. Also included are clear full-scale plans for cardboard or Plasticard supports to strengthen your model. The assembly instructions are extensively illustrated and very detailed.

Langleys also have a catalogue and the *Master Build Handbook* which is essential reading for anyone making scale houses.

They sell cast metal kits for baker's shops in either 1930s to 1950s or Victorian/Edwardian style, dressmaker's shops in Victorian and Edwardian style, a hardware shop in 1930s to 1950s style, an ironmonger's shop in Victorian/Edwardian style, a grocer's shop in 1930s to 1950s, Victorian or Edwardian style, a fishmonger or poultry shop in either 1930s to 1950s or Victorian/Edwardian, and a saddler's or motorcycle shop. Alternatively, you could use their pub kit to convert one of these buildings. The detail in these white-metal castings has to be seen to be believed. The ironmonger's shop, for example, is complete down to different styles of jug and saucepan, not to mention cleaning utensils. The dressmaker's shop has several styles of intricately detailed dresses. All my usual advice about painting white-metal castings applies.

Remove seam lines and other bits and pieces with a file or wet-and-dry paper. Prime well with spray paint and varnish your completed work for protection. It is easier to paint very small items by sticking them down on a piece of wood with Blu-Tack or masking tape, rather than attempting to hold them.

There are other suppliers of people and accessories for this scale, who can be found in the advertisements in magazines which cater for railway modellers. Wills have a workshop set, a blacksmith's and a set of farmyard junk – ladders, sacks, ploughs and other paraphernalia – as well as selling useful brick and stone card. Slaters Plasticard also sell a number of kits including a horse-drawn dray. Dart Castings sell a variety of suitable lamps: the gas lights which I have used came from this range and were bought at Pendon. Shire Scenes sell a delightful quarter scale bicycle kit which includes a delivery boy's basket. Cooper Craft Plastic Kits sell a variety of tools and also a set of ornate railway benches.

To paint brickwork and buildings and, indeed, to make buildings from scratch, there is no substitute for observing real buildings. The best products to use are opaque acrylics for undercoat with transparent colours for antiquing and subtle detail. An initial selection are Chinese white, grey (Davey's grey), dark grey or charcoal grey, raw sienna, raw umber, light red, cadmium red, cadmium yellow, ultramarine and terre verte or sap green. These are the names commonly used for artists' colours in tubes, in oils, watercolours and acrylics. Your local art shop would be able to recommend equivalents.

Most modellers are well aware of the ways in which bricks are laid. Commercial brick papers can be used, even in very small scales, but they never give the depth of three-dimensional modelling or the variations of colours found in old buildings. You can either scribe and paint the bricks yourself, or use a sheet product such as Slaters Plasticard or a kit such as the ones used for this project. Paint your bricks with an undercoat – I used car spray in grey – and then antique the whole model with a wash of dark brown or black transparent paint. The antiquing solutions sold by hobby ceramic suppliers are useful for this, but you can make up your own by adding water to any dark brown such as burnt sienna. Wipe back the initial wash before it has time to dry, leaving a dark colour in the crevices of the bricks. Brick colours vary from brick to brick across the wall: the basic colour is a light red or terracotta with traces of raw sienna, raw umber or grey added. Pendon sell a useful little pamphlet on arrangements of brick and brick colouring.

The final stage in painting your brick wall is to dry-brush. For this I use a small stiff ox-hair brush sold specifically for the purpose of dry-brushing by hobby ceramic suppliers. I load the brush with paint and then remove most of it on the side of my pallet, leaving the brush almost dry. This is a good way to add depth and colour and, indeed, patches of lichen and damp.

The paints for painting windows, doors and other fittings varies. I use Victorian- or Edwardian-style greens, blacks or browns. I find that gold, satin black, gloss black and dark green as well as the predictable white and cream are the most useful spray paint colours. Satin black is particularly good to represent cast iron whilst, with careful choosing, brown can be used for delicate woodwork. The dark greens are particularly useful for etched metal windows and also for Phoenix etched metal plants.

If you are nervous of using more sophisticated tools, most brass-etched kits can be cut with a pair of strong scissors or tinsnips. These small-scale projects survive better and can be kept cleaner if they are coated with a satin varnish after completion.

# GARAGE AND WORKSHOP

My garage workshop complex was made from a kit from Garden Railway Supplies which I have distressed by antiquing the brickwork. The punk rocker who owns the garage has been dressed in a Milliput boiler suit. The workshop at the side has been let to a sculptor based on a kind friend who went on trying to teach me to make life-size sculptures even when he knew that I was using what he taught me to make what he saw as toys. He is polishing an Anna Lamour Greek statue painted by me to look like lead. The other statues inside the workshop are from the same source. The two angels are from Tee Pee Crafts and have been hacked around to look like tombstone angels. Frontshop Shop Miniatures supplied the tools and the saucepan which I filled with glue to imitate polishing compound which, incidentally, smells disgusting. The two work benches came from a plastic bedroom set originally in pink. I spray-painted these a more subdued workshop grey. The peg boards are made of cross-stitch card. The sculptor's jeans are kitchen towel glued then modelled with a cocktail stick and painted dirty denim.

*Garage and workshop.*

# Bibliography

Adburgham, Alison, *Yesterday's Shopping, The Army and Navy Stores Catalogue* (David and Charles, reprint 1969).

Aitkinson, Sue, *Making and Dressing Dolls' House Dolls* (David and Charles, 1992).

Barham, Andrea, *Dolls' House Accessories, Fixtures and Fittings* (Guild of Master Craftsmen Publications, 1998).

Bolton, Vivienne, *The Doll's House Decorator* (Dorling Kindersley, 1992).

Cook, Clarence, *The House Beautiful* (Dover, 1995).

Dodge, Venus, *Doll's House Needlecrafts* (David and Charles, 1995).

Dodge, Venus and Martin, *Making Miniatures in ½ Scale* (David and Charles, 1989).

Dodge, Venus and Martin, *The Doll's House Do-it-Yourself Book* (David and Charles, 1982).

Eaton, Faith, *Classic Dolls' Houses* (Weidenfeld and Nicolson, 1990).

Forder, Nick, *Victorian Dolls' Houses* (Apple Press, 1996).

Gillon, Edmund, *The Picture Sourcebook for Collage and Découpage* (Dover Books, 1974).

Greene, Vivien, *Vivien Greene's Doll's House Collection* (Cassel, 1995).

Harris, Kristina, *59 Authentic Turn of the Century Fashion Patterns* (Dover Books, 1994).

Heaser, Sue, *Making Doll's House Miniatures from Polymer Clay* (Ward Lock, 1997).

Heaser, Sue, *Making Doll's House Dolls from Polymer Clay* (Ward Lock, 1999).

Innes, Miranda, *The Country Home Decorating Book* (Dorling Kindersley, 1989).

Johnson, Audrey, *Furnishing Dolls' Houses* (Bell, 1972).

King, Constance Eileen, *The Collector's History of Dolls' Houses, Dolls' House Dolls and Miniatures* (Robert Hale, 1993).

King, Pat, *Making Dolls' House Furniture* (Guild of Master Craftsmen Publications, 1993).

King, Pat, *Making Victorian Dolls' House Furniture* (Guild of Master Craftsmen Publications, 1995).

King, Roland, *The Quest for Paradise – A History of the World's Gardens* (Mayflower Books, 1979).

Lodder, Carol, *Making Dolls' House Interiors* (David and Charles, 1994).

Nisbett, Jean, *A Beginner's Guide to the Dolls' House Hobby* (Guild of Master Craftsmen Publications, 1997).

Peacock, John, *Fashion Source Books* (Thames and Hudson, various).

Peck, Tombi, and Dunn, Alan, *Modelling in Cold Porcelain* (Batsford, 1998).

Rice, Matthew, *Village Buildings of Britain* (Little, Brown, 1992).

West, Geoffrey, *Dolls' Houses* (The Crowood Press, 1996).

Yarwood, Doreen, *Fashion in the Western World* (Batsford, 1992).

Yarwood, Doreen, *The English Home* (Batsford, 1956).

The main book supplier to the trade is:

Lionel Barnard's Mulberry Bush
9 George Street
Brighton
BN2 1RH
e-mail: mulberry&pavilion.co.uk

A large selection of scholarly books on architecture and costume can also be obtained from Past and Present, tel: 01189 793853.

# DOLLS' HOUSE MAGAZINES

There is a number of dolls' house magazines published in the United Kingdom, the United States and the Netherlands. You will find that these carry advertisements for DIY supplies, craftsman-made products and dolls' house fairs. They are also a source of ideas and news of what is going on in the hobby. They also carry up-to-date advertisements for museums and dolls' house collections open to the public.

## BRITAIN

*Dolls House and Miniature Scene* (monthly; on general sale or by subscription)
EMF Publishing
7 Ferringham Lane, Ferring
West Sussex, BN12 5ND
Tel: 01903 244900
Fax: 01903 506626

*Dolls House Projects* is published four times a year by EMF Publications (address as above).

Each issue covers a single subject. There have been issues on gardens, weddings, Christmas, nurseries and interior decoration.

*Dolls House World* (monthly; on general sale or by subscription)
Ashdown Publishing Ltd
Avalon Court
Star Road
Partridge Green
West Sussex, RH13 8RY
Tel: 01403 711511
Fax: 01403 711521

*International Dolls' House News* (monthly; on general sale or by subscription)
Nexus Subscription Service
Tower House
Sovereign Park
Lathkill Street
Market Harborough
Leicestershire, LE16 9EF
Tel: 01858 435344 (credit card order line)

## UNITED STATES

*Miniature Collector* (bi-monthly; by subscription)
Ruth M. Keessen
Scott Advertising & Publishing Co.
Scott Publications Dept NO33
30595 Eight Mile
Livonia
Mi 48152-1798
Tel: 1-800-458-8237
Fax: 810-477-6795

*Nutshell News* (monthly; by subscription)
Kalmbach Publishing Co
21027 Crossroads Circle
PO Box 1612
Waukesha
Wi 53187
Tel: 1-800-533-6644 (subscriptions)

## THE NETHERLANDS

*Poppenbuizen & Miniaturen*
(quarterly; by subscription)
Posbus 84
5384 ZH Heesch
Holland
Tel: 04125 2331

# Suppliers

Andrew's Miniature World
16 Northumberland Place
Teignmouth
Devon
TQ14 8BZ
Tel: 01626 779672
(Dolls' houses and
supplies)

Anna Lamour
4 Central Place
Haltwhistle
Northumberland
NE49 0DF
Tel: 01434 320162
(Plasterwork)

Apollo Miniatures
31 Rayleigh Avenue
Wallington
Surrey
SM6 8HE
Tel: 0181 647 2091
(Whitewood furniture)

Artisans
7 College Road
Historic Dockyard
Chatham
Kent
ME4 4QW
Tel: 01634 828436
(Dolls' houses and
supplies)

Basique
87 Burnt Oak Broadway
Edgware
Middlesex
HA8 5EP
(Cake icing and cold
porcelain supplies)

The Bat's Wing
North Street
Alfriston
East Sussex
BN26 5UG
Tel: 01323 871433
(Dolls' houses)

Bits and Bobs Miniatures
Fairs only
Mouse families (formerly
sold by Perri's miniatures)
Tel: Janine 01903 210885
        Suzanne 01903 742231

Borcraft
Unit W25
Robin Mills Business
    Centre
Les Road
Greengates
Bradford
West Yorkshire
BD10 9TE
Tel: 01274 622577
(Wood and furniture)

Box Clever Miniatures
14 Chapel Street
Steeple Bumpstead
Suffolk
CB9 7DQ
Tel: 01440 730341
(Printed matter)

British Museum
46 Bloomsbury Street
London
WC1B 3QQ
(Rubber stamps, design
materials)

Brooklea Crafts
Orchard Cottage
10 Chapel Lane
East Huntspill
Highbride
Somerset
RN7 9BP
Tel: 01278 783798
(Furniture, work kits, half
scale cottages)

Bryan Frost
The Cottage
Great Underway
Coombe-St-Nicholas
Chard
Somerset
TA20 3NS
Tel: 01460 65271
(Half scale Tudor and
Georgian buildings)

Bryntor Pottery
102 Forest Road
Torquay
Devon
TQ1 4JX
Tel: 01803 311896

Carol Mann
1 Home Farm
Westhorpe
Southwell
Nottinghamshire
Tel: 01636 815461
(Pottery)

Cel Craft
Springfield House Gate
Helmsley
Yorkshire
YO4 1NF
(Cold porcelain, tools and
supplies for modelling)

Chicken Little Miniatures
Flat 1
39 Cranley Road
Guildford
Surrey
GU1 2JE
Tel: 01483 535307
(Wickerwork for dolls'
houses)

Clive Brooker
10 York Avenue
Stanmore
Middlesex
HA7 2HS
Tel: 0181 907 5701
(Pottery)

Coombe Crafts
The Coombes
Bishopstone
Swindon
Wiltshire
SN6 8PW
Tel: 01793 790479
(Craftsman-made dolls and
furniture, including half
scale)

Cove Models
119 Lynchford Road
Farnborough
Hampshire
GU14 6ET
Tel: 01252 544532
(Polystyrene models)

De MiniLaars
Straat 21
6913 AA AERDT
The Netherlands
(Icons, woodcarving, folk
painting, exhibiting at
Alexandra Palace and
Hove)

Denise Woods
47 Fox Hill
Bapchild
Sittingbourne
Kent
ME9 9AB
Tel: 01460 221622
(Furniture and furniture
kits)

Dijon Ltd
The Old Printworks
Streatfield Road
Heathfield
East Sussex
TN21 8HX
Tel: 01435 865108
(Importers and wholesalers
to trade)

Dixie Collection
4 Coney Hall Parade
Kingsway
Coney Hall
West Wickham
Kent
BR4 9JB
Tel: 0181 462 0700
(Mail order craft supplies)

The Doll Works
76 East Dulwich Road
London
SE22 9AT
(Dolls' house dolls, dressed
and kits)

Dolls' House Direct
Wern Newyd
Cwmpengraig
Velindre
Carmarthen
SA44 5HX
Tel: 01559 371578
($\frac{1}{2}$ and half scale houses)

Dollshouse Draper
PO Box 128
Lightcliffe
Halifax
West Yorkshire
HX3 8RN
Tel: 01422 201275
(Fabric supplies)

The Dolls House
    Emporium
Victoria Road
Ripley
Derbyshire
DE5 3YD
Tel: 01773 513773
(Assembled and kit houses
in $\frac{1}{2}$ scale furniture, dolls
and accessories)

Dolls of Distinction
Hunters Moon
Colchester Road
Wix
Essex
CO11 2RS
Tel: 01255 870834
(Half scale dolls)

Dolly Clobber
180 Bournemouth Park
  Road
Southend-on-Sea
Essex
SS2 5LU
Tel: 01702 68312
($\frac{1}{2}$ and half scale dolls)

The Enchanted Window
Carriage 5
Pleasure Island Train
St Anne's on Sea
Lancashire
FY8 1LY
Tel: 01253 726838
(Doll's houses)

Four Seasons Miniatures
48 Park Close
Heathersett
Norwich
Norfolk NR9 3EW
Tel: 01603 810346
(Polymer clay sculpture)

Freda Dorgan
Little Bramshaw
Old Bracknell Lane
East Bracknell
Berkshire
RG12 7AJ
Tel: 01344 421572
(Polymer clay dolls in $\frac{1}{2}$
and half scale)

Freestone Model
Accessories
28 Newland Mill
Witney
Oxfordshire
OX8 6HH
Tel: 01993 775979
(N and OO gauge railway
and allied supplies)

Garden Railway Supplies
Station Studio
Summerleys Road
Princes Risborough
Buckinghamshire
HP27 9DT
Tel: 01844 345158
(Half scale and G gauge
supplies)

Glasscraft
3 Willington Marina
Willington Quay
Wallsend
Tyne-and-Wear
NE28 6QT
(Miniature glass)

Gran's Attic
6 Church Walk
Stow Longa
Huntingdon
Cambridgeshire
PE18 0TW
Tel: 01480 860994
(Miniature supplies
including room boxes)

Halcyon
42b Fore Street
St Marychurch
Torquay
Devon
TQ1 4LX
Tel: 01803 314958
(Dolls' houses and
supplies)

Harrow Model Shop
190–194 Station Road
Harrow
Middlesex
Tel: 0181 427 6296
(Cars, boats, planes, war
games and military models)

HobbyCraft Art and Craft
  Superstore
Westway Cross Shopping
  Park
Greenford
Middlesex
UB6 0UW
Tel: 0181 747 7500
(Craft supermarket with
branches throughout the
country)

Hobby's
Knight's Hill Square
London
SE27 0HH
Tel: 0181 761 4244
(Mail order supplier of
craft materials including
dolls' houses)

Holly Products
Holly Cottage
Hassall Green,
Sandbach
Cheshire
CW11 4YA
Tel: 01270 761403
(Moulds, tools, books, for
cold porcelain)

Homecrafts Direct
PO Box 39
Leicester
LE1 9BU
Tel: 0116 251 3139
(Mail order craft supplies)

In Some Small Way
94 Station Road
Aldersholt
Nr Fordingbridge
Hampshire
SP6 3AZ
Tel: 01425 656003
(American folk art in $\frac{1}{2}$
and half scale)

It's A Small World
30 Princess Street
Yeovil
Somerset
Tel: 01935 41475
(Dolls' houses and supplies)

Jacksons Miniatures
6 Anderson Close
Epsom
Surrey
KT19 8LY
Tel: 01372 739363
(Plans, building supplies
and wallpaper including
half scale)

Jennifers of Walsall
51 George Street
Walsall
West Midlands
WS1 1RS
Tel: 01922 623382
(Mail order dolls' house
supplies)

JoJay Crafts
16 Copper Beech Close
Boxmoor
Hemel Hempstead
Hertfordshire
HP3 0DG
Tel: 01442 2267871
(Mail order dolls' house
supplies including a full
range of Phoenix)

Just-in-Case
8 Southfields
West Kingsdown
Sevenoaks
Kent
TN15 6LB
Tel: 01474 852115
(Mainly fairs – finished
goods including smaller
scales)

Lakeland Limited
Alexandra Buildings
Windermere
Cumbria
LA23 1BQ
Tel: 015394 88300
(Storage)

Langley Models
166 Three Bridges Road
Crawley
Sussex
RH10 1JT
Tel: 01293 516329
(White-metal castings for
buildings and accessories)

Les Chats
26 George Street
Ryhill
Wakefield
West Yorkshire
WF4 2DE
Tel: 01226 725829
(Horse-drawn transport)

Mack Fine China
454 Weston Road
Weston Coyney
Stoke-on-Trent
Staffordshire
ST3 62B
(Miniature china)

Maple Street
Wendy
Royston
Hertfordshire
SG8 0AB
Tel: 01223 207025/208937
(Dolls' houses and supplies)

Mary Jane Doyle
14 Woodbank Drive
Bury
Lancashire
BL8 1DR
Tel: 0161 797 7983
(Miniature knitting and
sewing supplies)

Masters Miniatures
4 Railway Cottages
Bridgerule
Holsworthy
Devon
EX22 7EB
Tel: 01288 381676
(Miniature antique
furniture)

Meadowcraft Miniatures
Unit 4B
Highfield Road Industrial
Estate
Camelford
Cornwall
PL32 9RL
Tel: 01840 213220
(Brass and nickel silver in
$\frac{1}{2}$ and half scale)

The Merry Gourmet
Lyndhurst
Beckford Road
Bathwick
Bath
Avon
BA2 6NQ
(Mail order supplies of food
and garden requirements)

Moorhen Miniatures
Threeways
Standon Lane
Ockley
Dorking
Surrey
RH5 5QS
Tel: 01306 627233
(Carpets in ½, half and
quarter scale)

The Mulberry Bush
9 George Street
Kemp Town
Brighton
Sussex
BN2 1RH
Tel: 01273 600471/493781
(Books)

North London Fabric
   Warehouse
38–40 High Street
Wealdstone
Harrow
Middlesex
HA3 7AA
Tel: 0181 863 6333
(Full size fabrics, trims,
starch spray and
haberdashery)

Ottervale China
8 Coleridge Road
Ottery St Mary
Devon
EX11 1TD
Tel: 01404 814498

Panduro Hobby
Westway House
Transport Avenue
Brentford
Middlesex
Tel: 0181 847 6161/01392
427788
(Mail order crafts and
miniature supplies)

Past and Present
19 Flamingo Close
Woosehill
Wokingham
Berkshire
RG41 3SJ
Tel: 0118 9793853
(Books and fine
miniatures)

Pendon Museum
Long Wittenham
Abingdon
Oxfordshire
OX14 4QD
Tel: 01865 407365
(Model museum with
useful shop)

Perma-Grit Tools
The White House
Pointon
Sleaford
Lincolnshire
NG34 0LX
Tel: 01529 240668

Peter Clark
2 The Ridgeway
Ware
Hertfordshire
SG12 0RT
Tel: 01920 464132
(Birds, animals, building
materials and fireplaces)

Prime Properties
14 Rackham Close
Cambridge
CB4 3HX
Tel: 01223 575936
(Houses and stalls)

Richard Stacey
The Workshop
Easthampnett Lane
Chichester
Sussex
PO18 0JY
Tel: 01243 533132
(Real brick, stone and slate
in ½ and half scale)

Robert and Renee Stubbs
Osprey Cottage
12 Pebble View Walk
Hopton-on-Sea
Norfolk
NR31 9SG
Tel: 01493 650633
(Dolls' houses and
craftsman-made furniture)

Rosie Duck Designs
40 Freshfield Street
Brighton
East Sussex
BN2 2YB
Tel: 01273 607374
(½ scale sculpture)

The Sculpey Lady
1 Bitterne Avenue
Tilehurst
Reading
Berkshire
RG31 4SP

Sid Cooke Dolls' Houses
Unit 1
CI Millsborough House
Ipsley Street
Redditch
Worcestershire
B98 7AL
Tel: 01527 595654
(Dolls' houses)

Squires Model & Craft
   Tools
100 London Road
Bognor Regis
West Sussex
PO21 1DD
Tel: 01243 842424

Sue and Alan's Little
   Treasures
The Cottage
Sibley Road
Hilldyke
Rishtoft
Boston
Lincolnshire
PE22 0RJ
Tel: 01205 310537
($\frac{1}{12}$ and half scale houses)

Tee Pee Crafts
28 Holborn Drive
Mackworth
Derby
DE22 4DX
Tel: 01332 332772
(Mail order egg-craft and
miniature supplies)

Tom's Miniatures
27 Carisbrook Close
Enfield
Middlesex
EN1 3NA
Tel: 0181 363 2958
(Houses and outbuildings
in $\frac{1}{12}$, half and quarter
scale)

Tony Knott
Chapel House
Chipping Norton
Oxfordshire
OX7 5SZ
Tel: 01608 641861
(Pewterware and bronze in
$\frac{1}{12}$ and half scale)

Trent Workshop
12 Deepmore Close
Alrewas
Burton on Trent
Staffordshire
DE13 7AY
Tel: 01283 790976
(Wood and wood finishing
supplies, at fairs and by
mail order)

Tudor Time Miniatures
Endersleigh
Bourton-on-the-Hill
Nr Moreton-in-Marsh
Gloucestershire
GL56 9AJ
Tel: 01386 700419
(Furniture)

Valerie Claire Miniatures
Oakville
Ashley Close
Tansley
Matlock
Derbyshire
DE4 5HX
Tel: 01629 58759
(Printed matter and shop
supplies)

Verlinden & Stok NV
Ondernemersstraat 4
KMO-Zone Mallekot
B-2500 Lier
Belgium
Tel: 03 480 65 26
($\frac{1}{32}$ and other military
supplies)

Victoria Fasken
2 Search Farm Cottages
Stourton
Warminster
Wilts
BA12 6QQ
Tel: 01747 840538
(Painted white-metal)

Wendy's Dolls
94 Tabors Avenue
Great Baddow
Chelmsford
Essex
CM2 7EN
Tel: 01245 474219
(Dolls including $\frac{1}{2}$ scale)

Wood Supplies
94 Colliers Water Lane
Thornton Heath
Surrey
CR7 7LB
Tel: 0181 689 1865

Some artists and suppliers
only attend fairs. While
every effort has been made
to ensure accuracy in this
suppliers' list,
circumstances change.
Readers should check the
dolls' house press for latest
details. Always telephone
before travelling or
sending money.

# INDEX